SOCIOLOGICAL INSIGHT

SOCIOLOGICAL
INSIGHT SECOND EDITION

An Introduction to
Non-Obvious Sociology

RANDALL COLLINS
University of California, Riverside

New York   Oxford
OXFORD UNIVERSITY PRESS
1992

Oxford University Press

Oxford   New York   Toronto
Delhi   Bombay   Calcutta   Madras   Karachi
Petaling Jaya   Singapore   Hong Kong   Tokyo
Nairobi   Dar es Salaam   Cape Town
Melbourne   Auckland

and associated companies in
Berlin   Ibadan

Published by Oxford University Press, Inc.,

198 Madison Avenue, New York, New York 10016-4314

Oxford is a registered trademark of Oxford University Press

Library of Congress Cataloging-in-Publication Data
Collins, Randall, 1941–
Sociological insight : an introduction to non-obvious sociology /
Randall Collins.—2nd ed.
p.   cm.   Includes bibliographical references and index.
ISBN -13 978–0–19–507442–0
1. Sociology—Methodology.
2. Sociology—Terminology.
3. Reasoning (Psychology)
4. Religion and sociology.   I. Title.
HM51.C594   1992   301'.01—dc20
91–28850

PREFACE

The aim of any discipline ought to be two things: to be clear and to be nonobvious.

Real knowledge ought to be communicable. It should be possible to say it so that it can be understood. And there should be something to say, something that makes a difference once you know it, something you didn't already know before.

Sociology has a bad reputation on both counts. It is infamous for abstract jargon. Sociological prose at its worst is considered virtually impenetrable. And once readers finally do penetrate the abstractions and the technicalities, all too often they find there was little being said. Sociologists seem to be saying what everyone already knows, documenting the obvious facts of our world, putting new names on the familiar. No wonder, it has been claimed, sociologists must hide behind a special language of their own making: if they said what they had to say in plain English, there would be nothing to it at all.

There is some truth to the allegations. Sociology has been needlessly obtuse at times, and a good deal of it has tended to be rather empty. The field keeps branching into new forms of technical jargon, ranging from the philosophical to the mathematical. Yet people, including some sociologists themselves, keep wondering if anything is being said.

Nevertheless, I think sociology has taken a bad rap. It may

be to a considerable extent its own fault. The smokescreen of concepts and definitions, the philosophical debates and the hyperextended methodologies, have covered up one important fact: there is a real core in sociology that has made some fairly significant discoveries. Sociology does know some important principles of how the world operates. These are not just matters of conceptualization and definition. They tell us why things happen in certain ways rather than in others, and they go beneath the surface of ordinary belief. The principles had to be discovered by professional scholars, including some of the major thinkers of the past; they are by no means obvious.

Since they are not obvious, there is no reason to dress them up in abstractions and technicalities. They are just as impressive stated in clear and simple language as they would be cloaked in an esoteric jargon. It is the test of real knowledge that it can be translated so that any intelligent person can see what it is about.

The core of this book is in the first two chapters. We begin with a central problem that distinguishes sociological analysis from most other, and more obvious, approaches to the world. This is the problem of the limits of rationality. It leads to a far from obvious conclusion: that the human power of reasoning is based on nonrational foundations, and that human society is held together not by rational agreements but by deeper emotional processes that produce social bonds of trust among particular kinds of people. Society is made up of groups. These groups are often in conflict with each other; but each group can operate only to the extent that each group is held together. That requires some nonrational mechanism producing common emotions and ideals.

What is this mechanism that generates social solidarity? The second chapter searches out the answer by examining another of sociology's unexpected findings, in this case concerning the nature of religion. Religion is a prime example of how certain forms of social interaction produce feelings of group ties. We find out something here about what religion actually means in people's lives, but we also discover something of wider significance. The theory of religion presented here is most important because it opens up a general theory of social rituals. These are key building-blocks for much of the rest of sociology; for rituals are little social machines that create groups and attach them to emotionally significant social symbols.

With these tools in hand, the following four chapters apply sociological analysis to a scattering of topics. Power and crime are areas where nonrational processes put a rather sharp limit on what people can understand and control by following ordinary rational calculations. Nevertheless, both power and crime have their paradoxical patterns, which we can understand from the point of view of a nonobvious sociology. The fifth chapter takes up the interrelated topics of sex, love, and the position of women in society. Here too we find social symbols on the surface, paradoxical structures in the depths. Here again the insights of a nonobvious sociology help us to see the direction in which patterns are changing in our own times.

The final chapter brings sociology into the space age. It shows that if we are ever going to build a computer with the intelligence of a human being, it will have to be programmed by sociologists. A real Artificial Intelligence capable of human creativity will need to have human emotions. The chapter brings us back full circle to the theories of rationality and rituals with which we began. If human rationality rests on a nonrational foundation of social rituals, then a computer can handle symbolism the way humans do only if it too can take part in ritual interactions.

What follows, then, is an introduction to sociology as a discipline that really does have something to say. In it I have sketched some of the most important arguments of Emile Durkheim and Erving Goffman, of Harold Garfinkel and Mancur Olsen, of Karl Marx and Max Weber, as well as the contemporary sociology of conversation and emotion.

Sociology has been pursuing an intellectual adventure that has taken us a long way beyond what is revealed by common sense. It should prove to be an entertaining expansion of our knowledge of the world. I have suggested a bit of the practical consequences of sociology as well. These include some of the more sophisticated ways that sociology points to in dealing with the issues of organizational power, crime, and sexual discrimination.

Sociology, of course, is by no means complete. Its theories are not all worked out; and there are considerable areas of genuine disagreement and much research yet to be done. I have not tried to cover all the topics and approaches in the field, although the reader will find mention of divergent theories at various points. Nor have I confined this book to expounding any one position. What it offers is a brief introduction to some of sociology's most interesting and elegant ideas. I hope it will whet the appetite for more.

Riverside, California   R.C.
August 1991

CONTENTS

SOCIOLOGICAL INSIGHT

1

THE NONRATIONAL FOUNDATIONS OF RATIONALITY

We pride ourselves upon our rationality. To be reasonable is a good thing; to be unreasonable is a sign of an idiot, a fool, or a small child. It seems obvious that the capacity to use reason is the most central item in our make-up. The human species is referred to technically as *homo sapiens:* we are the reasonable animal. We do things not by instinct but because we have reasons for them.

It would seem to follow, then, that pretty much everything we do is based on rational thought processes—the activities of everyday life, work and business, politics and government administration. A series of practical and academic disciplines exist to show the rational principles in each realm. Science and engineering govern our rational dealings with the physical world, economics with the activities of buying and selling, political philosophy and administrative science with the realm of policy decisions and formal organization. Even on the most personal level, a version of psychology describes individual behavior as straightforwardly determined by the pursuit of rewards and the avoidance of punishments. We are rational in any direction we might turn.

Against all this commonsense belief in rationality, however, sociology stands out as a dissenter. One of the central discoveries of sociology is that rationality is limited and appears only under certain conditions. More than that: society itself is ultimately based not upon reasoning or rational agreement but upon a non-rational foundation.

How can this be demonstrated?

The simplest reason for doubting the omnipotence of rationality is that different proponents of rationality often disagree among themselves. Different economists quite commonly present closely reasoned arguments for diametrically opposite positions. Politicians and administrators regard their own programs as highly rational, and those of their opponents as wrong. But those opponents have often had a chance to put these erroneous policies into action, very likely the last time the other party was in power. So even the proponents of rationality would have to admit that at least part of the time things were not determined by rationality but by its opposite. The question, of course, is which is which? The answer you get depends on which side you ask.

The existence of disagreements and conflicts is one reason to doubt the all-encompassing power of rationality. You may go farther and show that many policies, in themselves highly rational, can result in consequences that their own originators would regard as undesirable. A bureaucracy, for example, is designed to be a highly rational organization. Rational planning and accounting is precisely what makes an organization bureaucratic: experts plan for all possible contingencies; rules and procedures are laid down so that everything will be taken care of in the most efficient way; records are kept so that everything can be carefully accounted for. Actually, as most people know, paperwork can cause tedious delays, and the rules and regulations may be entirely inappropriate for the particular situation that comes up. Bureaucracies, designed for maximal efficiency, are notorious for their inefficiencies.

A good deal of sociology has focused on just this point. Max Weber, who formulated the theory of bureaucracy as an organization of record-keeping specialists using rational calculations, also saw that rationality can take several different, and opposing, forms. *Functional rationality* consists of following the procedures of coolly calculating how a result may be achieved most efficiently. This is in fact what we usually mean by rationality. But functional rationality is concerned only with the means to an end. *Substantive rationality,* on the other hand, considers the ends themselves.

The point was elaborated by Karl Mannheim, writing a few years after Weber's death in 1920. The same procedures can be *functionally* rational but lead to *substantively* irrational results. A bureaucracy consists of a network of specialists, who are concerned only with the most efficient means to achieve a particular goal. Just what these goals are is someone else's business, not theirs. This is why a bureaucracy can prove so frustrating for people who have to deal with it. Concerned only with their own duties, specialists consider anything that falls outside their particular province to be someone else's problem. Complaining to a bureaucracy is frustrating precisely because it is so easy for bureaucrats to evade responsibility. And this is not just a failure on the part of the individuals involved; it is the very rationality of the organization that results in the inability of bureaucrats to see the overall ends they are meeting or failing to meet.

One might suppose that it is the responsibility of the top-level administrators to see to the overall results. The problem is, the more bureaucratic the organization, the more the administrators themselves are trapped by their own machinery. They rely on the calculations and reports of specialists to tell them what is going on, and hence their view of the world is shaped by these same organizational procedures. The top executives see the world through the eyes of the accountants and engineers who report to them. As Mannheim argued, functional rationality tends to drive out substantive rationality. From this perspective, the governments of the twentieth century are prime examples of bureaucratic machinery running out of control. Within any government bureaucracy plans are carefully formulated and rationally carried out. Nevertheless, the results are often wastefulness and the creation of unforeseen problems in place of the old ones. Programs designed to reduce unemployment can produce inflation; regulations designed to increase safety can cause ruinous expenses and reduce productivity.

At the extreme, functional rationality can even threaten the very existence of civilization. For example, the carefully calculated and scientifically based preparations for military defense have resulted in an arms race that could easily culminate in total destruction by nuclear war. Mannheim, writing before World War II, did not foresee atomic weapons, but his point is particularly powerful because he shows the underlying organizational forms from which the arms race emerges. It is precisely the preponderance of functional rationality over substantive rationality that makes people unable to look ahead to the larger ends. Everyone concentrates on doing their own job, calculating the most efficient means to an end, acting as a cog in a larger machine. The purpose of the cog is to turn a particular wheel; the person who acts as the cog becomes unable to form any judgment about why the wheel should turn in the first place or whether it might not be better if the whole machine were scrapped and replaced with something else. Mannheim thus saw modern governments stumbling into wars willingly or not. It all happens because their own functional rationality makes it impossible to do anything else.

The irrational consequences of rational procedures are not confined to the military and political realms. The line of analysis begun in the nineteenth century by Karl Marx, and pursued in various forms by a number of modern sociologists, sees a similar dynamic in the economic realm. For the essence of capitalism, Marx pointed out, is precisely its tendency to reduce everything to calculations of profitability. In the process, human values are subordinated to economic ones, and the consideration of human beings becomes lost in the capitalist machinery. Furthermore, even the economic outcomes of the system are irrational in the long run. Marx saw the capitalist drive for profits resulting in crises of unemployment and business failure in which eventually even the capitalist class would be destroyed.

In Mannheim's terms, the *functional* rationality of capitalism is at the root of its *substantive* irrationality.

A number of different theories in sociology, then, focus on the unintended consequences of various actions that start out as rational in themselves. One might even say that the specialty of sociology is the study of processes that do not turn out to be rational. Nevertheless, in an important respect we are still on the surface of the problem. We have been dealing with examples of rational behavior that end up having irrational consequences. But there is also a more fundamental approach that shows that rationality itself is not the basis upon which society exists in the first place.

This analysis was formulated around the turn of the century by Émile Durkheim, a slightly older contemporary of Max Weber. In an important respect, modern sociology begins with Durkheim. He created the first university position in sociology in France and provided a good deal of the fundamental concepts and methods of sociology. It is worth pointing out, however, that certain aspects of Durkheim's theories are quite controversial today. Durkheim regards society as analogous to a biological organism in which every part contributes to the harmonious integration of the whole. This line of analysis, known as functionalism, tries to interpret each social institution as contributing to social order. Several schools of thought in modern sociology, including those that draw upon the intellectual traditions of Weber and Marx, reject Durkheim's functionalist approach. These schools stress instead the role of conflict and domination among social classes and other groups as prime determinants of the forms of social life. My own preference is to lean heavily upon Weberian conflict theory while incorporating (as Weber did) a number of ideas from Marx. Nevertheless, certain ideas of Durkheim remain absolutely central for sociological theory. These are his proof that society, and rationality itself, rest upon a nonrational foundation, and his theory of rituals as the mechanism by which group solidarity is created. In fact, as I will try to show, Weberian and Marxian conflict theories cannot really work unless they incorporate these Durkheimian ideas at their base.

In other words, I shall borrow part of Durkheim's theory but not all of it. This means separating Durkheim's microsociology from his macrosociology, using the former much more than the latter. Durkheim's macrosociology is his emphasis on the integration of the entire society as one big unit, which is precisely what Weber and Marx reject. Durkheim's microsociology is his theory of rituals in small groups. In my view, the overall structure of society is best understood as a result of conflicting groups, some of which dominate others. But conflict and domination themselves are possible only because the groups are integrated on the microlevel. Durkheimian theory is still the best guide to how this is done. Moreover, Durkheim's insights into rationality and rituals have been followed up by the most notable microsociologists of current sociology. Harold Garfinkel's ethnomethodology is in many ways another version of Durkheim's analysis of the nonrational foundations of rationality; Erving Goffman's studies bring Durkheim's theory of rituals to bear upon the details of everyday life.

In what follows, I shall trace Durkheim's proofs that society must rest upon a nonrational foundation, adding further evidence amassed by recent theorists. The next chapter presents Durkheim's theory of rituals. This shows not only how nonrational solidarity is created but also gives us a theory of *various kinds* of solidarity, which can explain a variety of different social forms. The theory originated in Durkheim's sociology of religion, but it extends far beyond this to topics such as politics and ideology. In the hands of Goffman, as we shall see, it develops into a theory of ritual in the secular, irreligious world of modern everyday encounters. This gives us some of the tools we need for analyzing, in later chapters, topics such as power, crime, and even the conflicts of sexual domination and liberation.

We will keep our eye on the fact that people pursue their own selfish interests at the same time that they have feelings of solidarity with at least some other people. Rationality and calculation, too, have their place in the scheme, along with their nonrational foundations. The key place to start, though, is with the Durkheimian theory of nonrational solidarity. This is one of sociology's most important nonobvious insights, a building block upon which much else rests.

THE PRECONTRACTUAL BASIS OF CONTRACTS

A traditional, rationalistic way of talking about society uses the concept of a social contract. "We, the people of the United States," begins the Constitution, "in order to form a more perfect Union, establish justice, insure domestic tranquility, provide for the common defense, promote the general welfare, and secure the blessings of liberty to ourselves and our posterity, do ordain and establish this Constitution of the United States of America." This refers to the founding of a government, but the idea is quite general. Political theorists like Hobbes and Rousseau saw the origins of human society in a contract made long ago by people deliberately banding together to follow common rules and reap the benefits of social cooperation. The actual event of making the original social contract in primitive times may be a metaphor, but the basic idea is intended quite realistically. People who are joined together in a society gain important things they cannot acquire alone, and hence it is a rational choice to form a society. Presumably we keep on reaffirming this rational choice as we see the benefits we get from upholding society and its rules.

Nevertheless, if we follow the logic of a strictly rational viewpoint, we come to the opposite conclusion. If people acted on a purely rational basis, they would never be able to get together to form a society at all.

This sounds paradoxical. Joined together, people can increase their economic productivity by a division of labor. Having formed a state, they can live under the protection of a rule of law and defend themselves against outside attack. It would ap-

pear, then, that the benefits of society are obvious, and that
rational individuals would see these benefits and form some kind
of social contract that provided for their cooperative existence.
Why shouldn't this obvious argument explain the existence of
society?

The trouble lies, as Durkheim pointed out, in the question
of just how a contract would be negotiated. For every contract
is really two contracts. One is the contract that we consciously
make—to establish a society, form a government, found an organization, agree to deliver goods at a certain price. That part
is easy enough. But there is a second, hidden contract: the implicit contract that you and your partners will obey the rules of
the first contract.

What does this mean? It raises the point that every realistic
businessperson, every shrewd politician, would be aware of: the
possibility that someone will cheat. To make it worthwhile to
enter into a contract, one must be sure that the other side will
uphold their part of the bargain.

What is more, if we assume that people are purely rational
individuals, who carefully calculate their possible gains and
losses, then it becomes impossible for either side to agree to a
contract. The rational individual, like a cynical politician, must
consider realistically what is likely to happen: the other side
may or may not live up to the rules of the agreement. Since the
other side may cheat, you yourself must rationally choose whether
to live up to the rules or not. And this calculation will make the
shrewd bargainer wary of any agreement.

Supposing you live up to your side of the bargain but the
other side cheats. What happens? You lose whatever you put
into it, and your partner gets something for nothing. The same
applies in the other direction. If you cheat and your partner
doesn't, then you get their contribution and put out nothing
yourself.

Purely rationally, therefore, you stand most to gain if you
cheat. If your partner is honest, you will gain everything and
lose nothing. If your partner cheats too, then at least you haven't

lost anything; neither side puts anything in, neither gets anything out, and you're back dead even where you started.

But what, you may ask, if both sides live up to the bargain? Don't they both benefit? Yes, but in that case no one gets something for nothing. There is an exchange; presumably both sides make some profit (although not always). If you compare this with the situation in which one side successfully cheats the other, you can see that you make much more profit by successfully cheating than by completing a deal in which both sides live up to their promises.

The bottom line, then, is: between cheating and keeping your promise, cheating is the more rational strategy. Cheating ensures that at worst you lose nothing and at best you gain a great deal. Keeping your promise, on the other hand, means that at best you gain a little while at worst you can lose a lot. The rational individual, thus, will always cheat.

If this were a completely rational world, no one would ever enter into a social contract and the world would consist of isolated individuals eternally suspicious of each other. Society would never get formed, though not because the presocial world is somehow savage and undeveloped, but precisely because it is *too* rational.

When Durkheim raised this argument, he did not mean to show that social organization is impossible. Obviously it is possible, since it exists. What he did mean to show was that social organization is not based ultimately on contracts. To the extent that now, in the modern world, contracts do exist—property contracts, business agreements, employment contracts, insurance policies and all the rest—it is because something exists underneath or prior to them. Somehow people have made that second, implicit contract to live up to the rules of the first, explicit contract.

Again, this is only a metaphor. What underlies our contracts is clearly not some other kind of contractual agreement. The same reasoning would apply to it as applies to the first contract. Would a rational, self-interested individual enter into a contract to uphold a contract? No, a rational person would have to expect that the other side would cheat on this contract, too, and would decide that the best strategy to follow would be to cheat first. So for the second, "deep" contract to hold good, there would have to be a third, still deeper contract—a contract to uphold the contract to uphold the contract. This obviously leads to an infinite regress. Once one starts questioning and calculating about just how one will come out of any agreement, there is no logical place to stop.

Durkheim concludes that contracts are based upon something nonrational. He calls this "precontractual solidarity." In effect, this means society is based on *trust*. People can work together not because they rationally decide there are benefits from doing so, but because they have a feeling they can trust others to live up to agreements. Society works precisely because people don't have to rationally decide what benefits they might get and what losses they might incur. People do not have to think about these things and that is what makes society possible.

So far, this may seem logically airtight. I have rationally shown that rationality can never establish social ties and that something beyond rationality must be invoked. Rationality points to its own limits. Fortunately, there does seem to be something beyond it. There is precontractual, nonrational solidarity, and that comes to our rescue.

Still, if we square this argument with what we know about the world, there are points that might make us uneasy. For one thing, it should be obvious that people get more from being in a successful cooperative organization than from working as isolated individuals. Society makes possible a division of labor; people working together can build houses, make roads, produce varieties of food, clothing, luxuries, and innumerable things that isolated individuals working alone could never accomplish. Why cannot the rational individual just look at this and make a rational decision to forgo cheating in order to reap the benefits of large-scale cooperation?

From the point of view of our rational model of exchange

this means that each individual should calculate not just the short-term payoffs from cheating or keeping a promise but also the long-term payoffs. If cheating seems more rational, that is because we have looked only at the short run. In the long run everyone has far more to gain by keeping their contracts operating smoothly. Even if there is only a small payoff for each transaction, over a long period of time this can build up to far more wealth and comfort than any cheater could gain from an isolated incident.

Nevertheless, I think that Durkheim's argument is on firm grounds. At any point along the line, individuals are going to be tempted to cheat. The more wealth there is in the pot—let's say it has been building up by a long history of successful cooperation—the more tempting it is going to be. And to be realistic here, as well as merely logical, we would have to say that the possibility of fraud is always with us, and the purely rational individual would always have to be on guard against it. Hence the calculating situation would come up over and over again, with the payoffs from cheating growing all the time. Rational individuals would know that these temptations would be seen by their partners as well as by themselves, and we are back in the same deadlock of mutual suspicions with which we began.

THE FREE-RIDER PROBLEM

There is a modern form of this argument that has been discussed a good deal in recent years. In this form, the question is not so much what makes society possible but, rather, once a society exists, how does it keep individuals attached to it? How does it make them contribute to the whole? The problem is that, left to their own rational self-interest, individuals take unfair advantage of contributions that other people make to the community as a whole.

Imagine a public bus service that is to be completely free. Everyone is asked to contribute to the cost of the bus, to chip in occasionally for gasoline, and to pay the driver. But the contributions are purely voluntary, and no fares are to be collected. Anyone can ride the bus whenever they want. People wouldn't have to worry about forgetting their wallets or having the correct change. The service would simply be available to everyone.

Now what would happen in this situation? Well, if people are going to be purely rational, they will calculate the costs and benefits of various courses of action. If no one contributes, of course, everyone would probably realize that there would be no bus service. So it is rational to want people to contribute to the cost of the bus. But notice, it is rational mainly to want *everyone else* to contribute, but not you yourself. The best deal is to be a free rider: get everyone else to pay for the community service while you ride free. Yet if everyone did this, the bus service would never be able to pay for itself.

The argument is not designed to show that this kind of idealistic community project is impossible, but rather that it cannot be done simply by relying on people's rationality. The fareless bus service could work if most people had a strong sense of unselfishness, or a feeling of duty, or were full of enthusiastic sentiments about the kind of free community they were making. The point is that these are transrational sentiments—emotions, moral feelings—and not rational calculations. This is true even if the proponents of such a reform might regard themselves simply as intelligent, rational people working out a plan from which everyone in the community would benefit. Certainly their plan may be rational—but only from the point of view of the group. The leap beyond rationality comes when you try to attach individuals to the group, to make them think of themselves simply as one group member among many others. Left alone, however, the rational thing for an individual to do is to encourage everyone else to act like a good citizen of the community, while he or she gets to be the free rider.

The fareless bus service may be only a hypothetical example, but there are many real-life instances of this problem. There was a famous murder, for instance, that took place in New York City while many people watched, but no one did anything about it.

The woman, named <u>Kitty Genovese</u>, was attacked at night while walking through a housing project. A man stabbed her with a knife, and she screamed for help. Dozens of people came to their windows in the nearby apartment houses. The attacker ran away. But then nothing happened. Kitty Genovese still lay wounded on the walkway. No one came to help; no one called the police. Eventually the murderer, who must have realized that no help was on its way, returned and stabbed her again. Presumably he did not want to be identified and decided to eliminate the key witness by finishing off the job.

The murderer seemed to be operating, at least by his final act, under cold-blooded rationality. The crowd of onlookers, safely behind their high windows, were presumably just cowards. This may be so, and it may also be true that they were displaying a very low degree of human sympathy and moral involvement by not bothering to call the police. But although these people did not act very admirably, it is not necessarily true that they were indifferent to the fate of the woman being murdered. Instead, they may all have been acting out a version of the free-rider problem.

There is some other evidence to back this up. Social psychologists have recreated the situation in a laboratory experiment. The key element in the situation was that there was a large crowd of people at the windows. They knew something was going on below, and what is more important, they knew that lots of other people knew it too. People looking out their windows could see other people at their windows. It was precisely because of this that no one went to help Kitty Genovese, and no one called the police: <u>everyone assumed that *someone else would do it*</u>. "After all," everyone may have reasoned, "why do it if someone else does? It only takes one phone call, and with all these people doubtless lots of others will already have done it by the time I get on the phone." The irony here is that everyone thought that way.

The spectators, then, were not necessarily totally immoral and unsympathetic but were only being rational about how to implement their morality. If you assume someone else has called the police, then your call contributes nothing and involves you in a slight inconvenience. Or supposing you were the first to call, then you would have to be interviewed as a police witness, asked questions for a report, possibly called to testify in court. If any of these people had been the sole witness of the attack on Kitty Genovese, most of them would probably have overridden these calculations about their own possible inconvenience and gone ahead and called the police. It is because of the self-awareness of the crowd of onlookers that people felt free to calculate these costs and benefits of doing it themselves as compared to letting someone else do it, i.e., precisely because everyone was reasonably certain that someone else would "pay for the bus," they felt entitled to be a moral free rider. Ironically, it was the peculiar structure of this crowd, seeing each other behind their closed windows, that sealed Kitty Genovese's death.

There are other, less melodramatic instances of the free-rider problem. One of them we see all around us, in the form of the trash that people throw on the sidewalks, in the parks and other public places. Why do people throw trash around considering that it makes the environment look so lousy for all of us? The main reason is probably the disproportion between the individual cause and the collective effect. An individual only discards a chewing gum wrapper or a paper cup; all by itself this small amount of trash is scarcely noticeable. What disfigures the landscape is the fact that large numbers of people throw their garbage out, and that adds up to a public mess.

Now look at the individual as a rational actor. A rational person knows that if no one threw trash, the streets would be a lot cleaner. But if you stop yourself from tossing that soft-drink can out the car window and dutifully wait until you find a trash can, it isn't going to make very much difference. By yourself, you really can't make public places look noticeably better, even if you are the kind of person who not only doesn't throw trash but goes around picking up trash that other people have left. Even if you want a better-looking world around you, it isn't really rational to refrain from throwing trash in public places. You simply can't achieve the goal as an individual, and so it is rational to give up and take the small convenience of not bothering to look for a trash can.

I am not making this argument, incidentally, in order to persuade people that it is all right to throw trash in public. Personally, I am glad that there are some people who don't and that some even go out of their way to pick up other people's trash. My point is that this meritorious behavior is not motivated by rationality but by something deeper: some kind of moral sentiment or maybe just an irrational phobia about messiness. Such phobias, as far as I am concerned, we should have more of. But we can't assume we can make the world a cleaner place just by convincing people rationally that they can do it as individuals.

What these examples demonstrate, in fact, is that a good deal of social life must be carried out in an explicitly organized, collective form or it can't be carried out at all. One way in which the free-rider problem is resolved is to not leave things up to individuals' free choice. Two ways in which the environment could be cleaned up, for example, are either to launch a moral crusade and generate a widespread emotional desire for cleanliness or to do it by action of a specific government agency. The former is not impossible, but it is hard to program or plan; we are fortunate that at various times there are tides of feeling rippling across the society that motivate people to care for their common environment. But such emotions cannot always be counted upon, and the more usual way to keep the streets and parks clean is for the government to hire people specifically to pick up the trash.

To put it another way, the free-rider problem can be overcome by not leaving things free. I don't know if the free bus service has been tried, but there was an analogous instance in Britain when socialized medicine was first introduced. All medical services were paid for by the state, and anyone could see a doctor anytime without charge. The initial result was an enormous increase in the frequency with which people went to the doctor. A great many complaints followed. Doctors felt swamped and declared that many people were coming in with dubious or no clear symptoms. This made services crowded for everyone, and dissatisfaction was widespread among the public users of the medical services. In other words, people were taking stock of the situation as individuals and decided they would get the maximum personal use of the free medical services, even if they didn't really need them and even if it resulted in a traffic jam at the doctors' offices that inconvenienced everyone.

Then the administrators of the medical system hit upon a solution. They instituted a small fee for each office visit, the equivalent of a dollar. The numbers of patients who appeared dropped off considerably, and doctors felt that once again they were seeing the normal range of medical complaints. Why did this happen? Basically what changed was that it was no longer a free-rider situation. Individuals now felt that they were back in a more normal situation, paying for medical services, and they began to calculate accordingly as to whether they really felt sick enough to incur the expense of seeing a doctor.

Oddly enough, this example points to the symbolic nature of these "rational" decisions. Whether something is "free" or not turns out to be more than a matter of real costs. From a strictly practical viewpoint, the fee charged was quite minimal, and virtually anyone who was genuinely ill would still find the service a bargain at this price. It appears, rather, that the idea of being a free rider is by and large irresistible for most people, if the collective provides something without attaching any responsibility for using it in a way that safeguards the rights of other people to use it too. (The same sort of thing has been noticed in wars: it has often happened that soldiers will go without fresh rations for days because of supply difficulties; then when supplies finally get through, they waste a good deal of their now-abundant food instead of saving it for other troop units that might be in the same condition they were in yesterday.) As long as the state was providing medical services absolutely free, no one felt any compunction about squandering them. But as soon as they had to pay even a nominal fee, they no longer seemed to have this attitude of "getting something for nothing, and everyone else be damned."

It is even possible to suggest that this tells us something about the symbolic nature of money. A few coins, after all, mean very little as far as economic exchange goes. But this token amount can nevertheless make the difference between "free" and "paid for," which can trigger an entirely different way of approaching social relationships. In fact, money may be symbolic in this way a good deal more than we realize. The value of being frugal does not often add up to very much objectively, e.g., you usually save very little by checking all the differences in pennies between the canned goods at the supermarket, especially if you blow far more than the difference at a restaurant or the movies. Ironically, people find it easier to be frugal about small matters than about large ones, such as buying a house or a new car, which can negate everything that one can save at the supermarket in years. But socially, this kind of small-scale frugality does make sense. Because you buy small goods so much more often than large ones, you have far more chances to exercise your sense of control over market prices in that way than in a one-shot deal involving some much more expensive item.

As in so many things, it is our subjective feelings about the world that count, more than the objective value of practical payoffs that we receive. Even when we do calculate, it may be only a symbolic calculation, expressing an uncalculated feeling that it is good to calculate. Ultimately, what holds society together is not the calculations but just these sorts of deeper sentiments.

THE RISE OF CONTRACTUAL SOCIETY

A follower of Durkheim could also appeal to the historical facts. If we stick, say, to economic contracts, the fact is that successful business contracts are a relatively recent innovation. Business dealings in traditional societies were carried out either in a highly ceremonial and distinctly noneconomic fashion or else with a very high level of suspicion. On the one hand, there were traditional systems of trade between particular families, or ceremonial objects, which circulated among different tribes in a prescribed manner. Here there was plenty of trust but little real economic calculation. A certain household had to deliver a basket of yams to their in-laws on a certain festival day and received back a basket of fish upon the birth of a child. It was this sort of tradition that made up much of tribal economics and not really buying and selling; there was no encouragement at all to increase productivity or devise new products.

On the other hand, in societies like medieval Europe or China, there were real economic transactions. Long-distance traders would arrive with goods that were produced not for subsistence but in order to make a profit. This constituted a real market; but since the partners to transactions were strangers to one another, they carried out their dealings with a high degree of suspicion on both sides. Everyone wanted to have goods in hand before they delivered the cash, and no one in their right mind would have extended any kind of credit without taking extreme precautions. It is for this reason that ancient and medieval societies around the world could not produce a modern-style capitalist industrial society.

Generally speaking, these societies were not held back by lack of the material resources for economic productivity. One cannot say, either, that the medieval Chinese or Italians or the ancient Greeks were not rational enough to see that they stood more to gain by being less suspicious and more willing to make long-term contracts. On the contrary, from our viewpoint these merchants were excessively rational. They were concerned about the long-term profits and losses as well as the short-run balance. If somehow a modern American suddenly appeared before them and repeated the argument of the paragraphs above, they would undoubtedly reply that if they weren't suspicious they would lose even more money in the long run. And they would have been right.

The clincher is that when a modern contractual economy did

come into being, it happened precisely in the way that Durkheim's argument would predict. It took the creation of new bonds of trust to make it possible. The rise of capitalism was certainly a shift away from the ultrasuspicious dealing of the Middle Ages. Businesspeople began to emphasize a slow, steady accumulation of small profits, repeated over and over again across many transactions, and that meant living up to the terms of their contracts. Long-term contracts began to replace the shady bargaining and one-shot deals of the medieval merchants. It was this that made mass production practical. What good is it to have machinery turning out large numbers of items if there is no way of selling them? It is not industrial technology that made possible the modern economy, then, but this shift in the way in which business was carried out that made possible the technological developments of the industrial revolution.

What is crucial for my argument is the fact that this shift to a highly contractual society went along with a change in the realm of "precontractual solidarity." The capitalist takeoff and the industrial revolution were accompanied by a religious revolution. This leads us to a famous argument of Max Weber concerning the way in which the Protestant ethic affected the spirit of capitalism. This is actually a more complex theory than it is usually taken to be, but the only point that need detain us is that the Protestant type of religious morality motivated businesspeople to be honest, to stop cheating their customers, perhaps even to cease being concerned with purely worldly profits. The religious revolution, in short, created pockets of trust within a society that had long been used to an atmosphere of economic distrust. It was in these pockets that a new, contractual economy could build up and eventually spread to take over the world.

POWER AND SOLIDARITY

Opposition to the Durkheimian argument ought to be fading at this point, but there is at least one more possible rejoinder. Yes, you may agree, it is true that contracts cannot be upheld

purely by the self-interest of the individuals involved. But why
fall back on some mysterious solidarity or feelings of trust? All
that is really needed is something to enforce contracts in the
event that they are broken. If someone cheats, you can always
take him or her to court; if something is stolen, you can have the
thief arrested. You can rationally have faith in contracts because
you know that they can be enforced. So it is not some irrational
emotion that makes contracts possible but the existence of the
courts and the police.

Now this isn't a bad answer. The pure Durkheimian argument seems to hang in the air in a kind of perfect abstractness.
If you bring it down to earth, of course, you have to admit that
there are courts and police in the world. Anyone who has ever
been involved in business, or in the legal professions, knows
that people still cheat today, in our highly contractual society,
and regularly get hauled into court because of it.

Moreover, this argument has the merit of filling in many important details of the way in which capitalist society emerged
historically. Weber, after all, was not just concerned with the
Protestant ethic; he also paid a great deal of attention to the
way in which the legal system developed along with the structure of the modern state, the police, the army, and all the other
agencies by which social order can be enforced. Only when
courts and governments could be organized to enforce business
contracts could capitalism take off. The foundation of modern
capitalism is not just religion but the state. Precontractual
solidarity, it would seem, is not really a matter of trust but a
matter of force. People live up to contracts because they have
to, whether they want to or not.

This is a hard-nosed and realistic argument, and it makes us
pay attention to some crucial parts of social history that we
might otherwise tend to ignore. Nevertheless, although it pushes
it one step further back, it leaves the Durkheimian argument
intact. Suppose we admit that the state upholds the law of contracts. What upholds the state? The state after all is a social organization; it coordinates people who have agreed to work to-

gether to accomplish some political end. Why should the people who make up the state adhere to the contract among themselves? This puts us back where we started. Why should the officials of the state obey orders considering that it would be more reward-ing to cheat on this too and follow their own interest? And, of course, assuming the other officials are rational individuals too, you would expect that they also will cheat and try to take advan-tage of you. On purely rational grounds there is no reason why the state should hold together, any more than anything else. So the state cannot back up social contracts unless the state itself rests on some kind of precontractual solidarity.

There is one last line of defense against this argument. You could say that the members of the state—the officials, the police, the soldiers in the army—obey orders because if they don't the force of the state will punish them. Now this is true, but only because the state already exists today. But how was it possible to create such an organization? The coercive arm of the state can certainly exert tremendous force against the individual, but it is strong only as long as the state exists, i.e., only as long as the contract to obey orders holds among the people who make up the state. Here again historical and contemporary reality shows just how little one can take this for granted. States and armies break apart when people in them stop thinking of them-selves as members of the group and think only of their own individual self-interest. It is when the army thinks "every man for himself!" that they are about to panic into full retreat. When everyone in a state thinks that way, the state is on the verge of revolution.

For this reason, we are forced to admit that the state is held together in the same way as any other social organization: by some kind of precontractual or nonrational solidarity. Weber described the basis of the state as its *legitimacy*. This is not a rational calculation of self-interest but a belief that the state is valid and powerful. Legitimacy may exist only in people's minds, but if it does exist there, then it makes the state powerful. When the state is powerful, it can force people to obey and this in turn makes it even more legitimate. The whole process turns on itself full circle. An irrational belief in the state, whatever its foundation, creates its own reality. Although rational individuals could never get together and create a state purely by making a contract, people who share a common sentiment provide the basis for a state whose powers can coerce everyone.

This does not mean that everyone has to feel solidarity with each other in order for a state to exist. The government might well be a military dictatorship or perhaps the temporary rule of a particular political party. The basic nature of politics is disagreement and struggle among various factions. But the key point is that *no particular faction would be able to dominate others if it lacked solidarity in its own ranks.* For a group to have this solidarity, its members must stop calculating their own self-interest vis-à-vis each other and feel only their common interests as a group. This requires that somehow they share a nonrational sentiment that makes them want to contribute to the group instead of being free riders. It is for this reason that ideologies, symbols, and emotions are so important in politics.

It would be a mistake to conclude that all of society is one big mass of perfect solidarity. On the other hand, it would be an even bigger mistake to assume that nothing exists but calculating, self-interested individuals. As we have seen, if everyone were solely calculating all the time, social groups would not exist at all; there would be very little for self-interested individuals to fight and connive about. There would be no state for dictators to rule, no wealth for embezzlers to steal, no trust to abuse.

What we need to recognize is simply that nonrational sentiments are crucial in any organization; *but the extent and strength of these sentiments are variable.* Just because individuals feel solidarity toward some people in some groups does not mean they feel it toward everyone. Sentiments of trust among members of a family will suffice to hold a family together (and those sentiments do not have to occur all the time—part of the time will do, leaving plenty of room for quarrels within the group). If the world were made up of only families like this, they would live in little pockets of internal solidarity, with considerable distrust among them externally. In fact, numerous historical societies have taken that form. In another form there may be solidarity only within the military regime that constitutes a state, ruling over a subjugated populace that has no trust whatever in its masters. That is another type of society, and history has seen all too much of it as well.

I could go on and on with the variations. The capitalist economy, with a rather widespread form of trust in certain kinds of economic contracts, is yet another version. Here, people have enough trust so that they will put their money in someone else's hands to invest it; they will work expecting that they will be paid for it at the end of the month; they will accept pieces of paper promising to pay out a sum of money from a checking account. These and myriad other little acts of trust make possible a gigantic economic machine. It is obvious, too, that this society is full of conflicts and has its own occasion for distrust. But in an ironic way, the distrustful occasions basically depend upon the trustful ones. It is because people put their money in banks that there can be bank robbers; it is because most people are willing to accept on faith the value of a piece of paper that money can become the object of the complicated deals of financial speculators.

Sociologists do not give up on explaining any of this. They aim to show just exactly when and how class conflict works, why crime occurs, and all the rest. They are interested in both solidarity and conflict; and in fact, it is impossible to explain one without the other. They are also concerned with why some societies are enclaves of little feuding families while others have large economic networks or dictatorial states. The calculating, self-interested individual has a place in all this. But such individuals are never very effective unless they can relate to nonrational feelings of solidarity that hold groups together.

An individual can dominate other people mainly by taking advantage of their feelings of solidarity. Whoever can convince

others that he or she is really one of them has a better chance
of taking advantage of them. The most successful exploiter is
the one who makes others feel that he or she has their best interests at heart. This means making an appeal precisely on that
level and through those mechanisms by which nonrational sentiments of solidarity operate. This is a fundamental weapon of
dictators, con-artists, politicians, and perhaps everyone who
wishes to pursue their own self-interest aggressively in society.
Feelings of solidarity are often called out in people, deep beneath their own rational calculation of self-interest. Whoever
knows how to arouse these feelings in others has a crucial
weapon, to use for good or evil.

If self-interest individuals need to be concerned with solidarity, this is even more true for self-interested groups. Groups
that are in conflict with other groups can only come to exist in
the first place if they are held together internally. Solidarity and
conflict are not mutually exclusive; solidarity is a crucial weapon
for whoever wants to gain some advantage over someone else.
The best-organized group usually wins, and that means the
group with the most internal solidarity.

The Marxian theory of class conflict has recognized this too,
in a way. For Marxists, a key question has been how people,
especially the working class, can be organized to fight effectively
for power. Usually this has been described as the problem of
creating "class consciousness," i.e., having individual workers
become aware of their interest as a group. The problem, however, is by no means a simple one. People's feelings of solidarity
do not automatically line up into two sharply divided groups
of capitalists and workers. A good deal of the time people may
act as purely self-interested individuals, e.g., different businesses
are by no means allies when they are competing against each
other for the same market, and workers are not unified if they
are competing for a particular job or a promotion.

Nevertheless, under particular conditions these disputes
among individuals are put aside and groups do form. But how
many groups will there be? The magic number two does not

come up so very often. Frequently there are many different business interests—bankers versus industrialists versus retailers versus exporters versus farmers—and it is the complex jockeying for favors that makes up so much of ordinary politics. Similarly, workers may form into trade unions, but the different unions may well be at odds with each other. The teamsters may be in conflict with the auto workers; union members may monopolize jobs, making them inaccessible to nonunion workers. Female workers may be discriminated against by male workers, and the same may happen among white, black, and ethnic groups.

The problem for the Marxist theorist is not that there is too little class conflict in the world but that there is too much. There is not just conflict of workers versus capitalists. In the socialist societies, there are conflicts between workers and bureaucrats, faction fights among communist party members, army, and secret police. Social scientists have known this for a long time, and the whole world became aware of it after 1989 with the sudden revolt of Eastern Europe, and the outburst of chaotic struggle in the USSR. As socialist societies fall apart, capitalist societies look good to most people by comparison. But the moment of excitement should not blind us to the fact that all societies, including our own, are full of conflicting groups at various levels of intensity. As the German sociologist Ralf Dahrendorf pointed out, any situation of power between people who give orders and others who take orders leads to the potential for conflict. Every modern social structure contains the potential for struggle between power classes. Worse yet, ethnic, racial, and religious identities are full of dangerous energies, ready to struggle for predominance, and sometimes to massacre each other. This dismal force of ethnic and religious violence has been released by the collapse of the Soviet power in its own Republics and in Eastern Europe. We also see terrible examples of its destructive power in India, the Middle East and elsewhere. In the United States, ethnic and religious issues are smouldering today rather than burning, but here too arguments and insults sometimes turn into bullets and firebombs.

For sociologists, conflict and solidarity are two sides of the same coin. Groups often have the most solidarity within when they are mobilized against an enemy without. Conflict leads to solidarity of at least some groups, and vice versa. What we aim to show is why the whole range of different group line-ups exist at various times. When do large numbers of competing groups exist—be they economic and occupational groups, racial and ethnic groups, families, political parties, or social movements? When do these boil down into lineups of only a few groups? Does total solidarity of all groups ever occur so that there is only one group, and if so, under what conditions? And at the opposite extreme, when do isolated individuals detach themselves entirely from any group bonds and pursue only their own self-interest?

These problems are by no means all solved by sociological theory. But some of the crucial mechanisms by which these events take place, I believe, are understood. The central lesson, as argued in this chapter, is that group organization does not depend on rational calculations. It is not, as Marx thought, that groups are formed when people become *conscious* of their common interests. The consciousness and interests are only the surface of things. What is beneath the surface is a strong emotion, a *feeling* of a group of people that they are alike and belong together.

This is not to say that the interests aren't real. But the reason I say they are on the surface of things is that people have all sorts of interests, some of which bring them together with others, some of which divide them. A doctor is a medical association, for example, "obviously" has an interest in joining with other doctors to monopolize the income from practicing medicine; at the same time, it is equally in that particular doctor's interest to compete with other doctors for patients. The same kind of thing can be said for workers in a trade union or members of any other group. And this dilemma operates as groups must choose whether to compete with other groups or to join them; it is equally in the interest of a trade union to compete with other unions for preferred treatment as it is to join together to fight for the interests of all workers. Rational interests simultaneously attract and divide people. And the free-rider problem is always with us, tempting individuals to make their own best deal at the expense of other members of their group.

Which interests win out, nonetheless, is not a matter of rational calculation. It depends on something deeper: on _moral feelings that bind people together in a group_. The procedures that produce these moral feelings, I am going to argue, are _social rituals_. When such rituals have done their work and group solidarity is created, the interests that people hold in common in that group take on a new status. The interests become moral rights and become surrounded with a kind of symbolic halo of righteousness. From another perspective this might be called ideology. The key point is that groups not only contend over competing interests, but they also always see their own interests in _moral_ terms. As we shall see, if they did not they could not even exist as groups.

Whether we are looking for the basis of class conflicts or of the solidarity that underlies a contractual society, then, we come down to the question of why some people feel that they can trust others. Durkheim showed that these feelings of trust cannot depend on rational calculations, but must have a deeper, unconscious source. And having raised the problem, Durkheim proceeded to offer a solution, his theory of social rituals. This will be the topic of the next chapter.

2

THE SOCIOLOGY OF GOD

There are two obvious positions that you can take about religion. Either you believe it or you don't: in one case it is a supreme Reality that transcends everything sociology is concerned with; in the other it is an irrational superstition about things that don't exist.

For the most part social thinkers have taken the second of these two attitudes. Utilitarians and rational reformers in general tended to look on religion as an archaic, irrational force. It is the source of superstition, beliefs about an invisible world of spirits and ghosts. Legal reformers saw religion as an institution of Inquisitors and heresy-hunters, burning people at the stake for their beliefs or under the mistaken judgment that they were witches. Radicals saw religion as the upholder of the status quo, a kind of agency of the ruling class that made people put up with economic and political injustice in return for a promised life in heaven after they die. Rational intellectuals, generally seeing no grounds for believing in theological dogma, regarded religion as a relic of the Dark Ages, something that would eventually die away as societies became modernized.

For a while, this prediction seemed to be coming true. Certainly religions lost most of the hold they had over people just a few centuries ago. Witch-burning no longer took place, and belief in malevolent spirits largely disappeared. Churches became less dogmatic and more tolerant. Adherence to religion declined. People no longer attended daily mass or sat through protracted Sabbath-day sermons. Eventually we seemed to be reaching the point where not only were the stores open on Sunday morning, but people were just as likely to watch a football game or play golf as go to church. The church lost its power to prohibit people from doing such things and seemed to be losing its power to motivate other aspects of people's lives as well. Similar trends could be found around the world. As traditional tribal and agricultural societies came into the modern orbit, their various religions also began to lose their power. One might have expected that religion would fade away entirely.

But this has not happened. Religion in the United States is far from dead. Even here, where science and technology has advanced to very high levels, and education is more widespread than anywhere else in the history of the world, the expectations of religion crumbling under the advance of rationality has not panned out. Instead we see religious revivals of many sorts. There has been a new movement of vehemently fundamentalist Christianity, which takes the Bible as literally true and denounces what it regards as the moral failings of the contemporary world. This religion has not merely defended itself passively but has taken the offensive and entered into current politics in an effort to win back the old compulsory powers of the church. Simultaneously, Oriental religions have made a greater influx into Western societies than at any previous time. Followers of Krishna, Hindu gurus, and Buddhist monks have appeared in large numbers, while Islam has made its appeal especially among the black populace. Astrology and the occult have attracted widespread interest and permeate the mass media. Some of these same kinds of religious and occultist movements have appeared over and over again in modern times. Obviously the prediction of a steady trend toward total secularization and rationalism is incorrect.

What is most significant about religion for a sociologist, however, is neither of the two obvious stances regarding it, either favoring or opposing religion. There is a third alternative. Durkheim created a nonobvious theory of religion, in which the key to religion is not its beliefs but the social rituals that its members perform. Religion is a key to social solidarity, and religious beliefs are important, not in their own right, but as symbols of social groups. Religion thus becomes sociologically important as a prime example of a nonrational phenomenon playing a major role in social life. The analysis of religion, moreover, leads us to a very important general theory that enables us to understand social rituals and the way in which they create both moral feelings and symbolic ideas. This theory has applications far removed from the realm of religion itself. It helps us to explain politics and political ideologies, and the dynamics of solidarity that make conflicts possible among social groups. It even tells us something about the private secular realms of modern life. You do not have to be either religious or politically active to experience the relevance of social rituals. They permeate modern life, just as they did any other time in history. It is only the forms and arrangements of rituals that has changed. Thus I will trace out the varieties of social ritual, from Durkheim's sociology of religion to Goffman's sociology of everyday life.

It is no accident that the same theory should tie together the bizarre practices and beliefs of primitive religion with the taken-for-granted behaviors of modern life. For if society is possible only on a nonrational foundation, then even our self-consciously rational thought of today must rest upon some nonrational processes. This is precisely what the theory of social rituals helps explain. Unravelling the nature of the gods, sociologists have found an explanation of the rituals and symbols without which social groups of any kind would not be possible.

THE COMMON BASIS OF RELIGIONS

Durkheim's basic assumption is that religion represents something real. Personally an atheist, he saw no reason to believe that some transcendent, supernatural God existed, let alone the multiplicity of gods and goddesses, angels, devils, demons or spirits in which people of various religions have believed at one time or another. Nevertheless, how could people have been in error for such a long time, throughout most of history in fact? How can these sorts of beliefs continue to hold sway among large sectors of the populace even today? Something in which people have believed so strongly could hardly be based upon nothing but a mistake in reasoning. There must be something that corresponds to these religious beliefs, something real that people have symbolically seen in the guise of the gods. Though the reality that the gods represent is not what its believers claim it to be, it does have the symbolic force of something very strong. People have always regarded the spirits or the gods as more powerful than ordinary humans. What religion represents, then, must be something much more powerful than the individual.

How would you go about proving what it is that religions represent? The first step is to compare. What is it, we ask, that all religions have in common? Not any particular doctrine of God—not Jehovah and Jesus, Allah and Mohammed, Krishna, Vishnu, Isis or Zeus. Not necessarily the concept that there is a single god, for there have been many religions with more than one: the good and evil pair of Ahuramazda and Ahriman of the Zoroastrians, the pantheon of ancient Greek and Roman gods dwelling upon Mount Olympus, the many gods and goddesses of the ancient Hindus, and numerous others. Not even the mere concept of *any* god: Buddhism, for example, is obviously a religion, but its basic concept of Enlightenment is completely atheistic. And in many tribal religions, there are no gods, though there are totem animals, plants, rocks, and so forth that constitute the object of the cult.

What all religions have in common, rather, are two things: certain beliefs held by all adherents and certain rituals that the believers collectively perform.

The basic religious belief is that the world is divided into two categories: the *sacred* and the *profane*. Things that are *sacred* can be anything: spirits, invisible gods, particular animals or trees, altars, crosses, holy books, special words that only the initiated can speak or songs that only they can sing. The distinctive thing about the *sacred* is that it is dangerous and supremely important: you must approach it seriously, respectfully, and with due preparation. *Profane* things, on the other hand, constitute the rest of the world: all the other things that you can deal with matter-of-factly, with whatever mood you wish, and for whatever purpose you find useful or desirable.

This is the basic religious belief: the dualism of sacred and profane. Along with it goes the basic religious action, namely, *ritual*. A ritual is very different from ordinary behavior. An ordinary practical action, such as walking down the street, doing your work, shopping for something at the store, or whatever, can be done in a variety of ways. It makes no difference how you do it as long as you get the job done. Ritual, on the other hand, is very strictly determined behavior. In rituals, it is the forms that count. Saying prayers, singing a hymn, performing a primitive sacrifice or a dance, marching in a procession, kneeling before an idol or making the sign of the cross—in these, the action must be done the right way. Rituals are not a means to an ulterior end, the way practical actions are; you cannot say it makes no difference how you do it as long as the goal is attained, for the form of the ritual is its own end. It is meaningful if it is done right and worthless if done wrong.

Thus, religions are made up of beliefs and rituals, and the two are connected. Rituals are procedures by which people must conduct themselves in the presence of things that they believe to be sacred. The opposite of these two go together as well: ordinary, nonritual behavior is how you act in the presence of the profane. As we shall see, Durkheim gave priority to rituals over beliefs. In a certain sense, the correct performance of the ritual is what gave rise to the belief in the sacred.

The question now arises: how could people have ever invented this distinction? Why has there been this near-universal tendency to divide the world into the sacred and the profane? Nothing in nature suggests it. Animals do not make the distinction. Everything in the physical world is on the same level. Why should people imagine that it is filled with invisible spirits, gods, forces that demand certain kinds of arbitrary respect and that are dangerous if disobeyed? There are real dangers in the world, to be sure, but people must have very quickly learned how to deal with them in practical ways. From a purely physical viewpoint, religion seems to have filled the world with hallucinations.

But there is one reality that does have all the characteristics that people attribute to the divine. It is not nature, nor is it metaphysical. It is *society itself*. For society is a force far greater than any individual. It brought us to life, and it can kill us. It has tremendous power over us. Everyone depends upon it in innumerable ways. We use tools and skills we did not invent; we speak a language passed on to us from others. Virtually our whole material and symbolic world is given to us from society. The institutions we inhabit—our form of family life, economy, politics, whatever they may be—came from the accumulated practices of others, in short, from society. This is the fundamental truth that religion expresses. *God is a symbol of society.*

Thus it is not an illusion to feel that something exists outside of ourselves, something very powerful, yet not part of the ordinary physical reality that we see with our eyes. Moreover, this something—the feeling of our dependence upon society—exists simultaneously outside and inside ourselves. In religions there is always a connection between the sacred world beyond us and something sacred inside ourselves. God is simultaneously without and within. In the advanced religions such as Christianity or Islam there is the concept of the individual's soul, which belongs to God. In the totemistic religion of primitive tribes there is a similar connection, for every member of the tribe is also identified with the totem. If the sacred animal of an Australian clan is the kangaroo, then every clan member feels that in some way they too are kangaroos. This belief, too, corresponds to something real. We are parts of society: it only exists in the aggregate because of us.

More than that, our inner selves are constructed out of parts that come to us from without. Our name, our self-identity, come from the ways we relate to other people, and from the way they relate to us. We usually think of ourselves by our own names, but we seldom created these names for ourselves. Even if you were to change the name given by your parents, you may find that you are known by a nickname given by other people. And the deeper aspects of our self-image come even more powerfully from our experiences with other people. Do you think of yourself as good-looking, plain, or downright hideous? Do you feel confident, controlled, spontaneous, anxious, or harried? Successful or unsuccessful? These feelings about yourself are for the most part formed by the way in which other people have treated you. This dependence of the self-image upon other people is well known in social psychology. We tend to see ourselves through the eyes of other people. To express this fact the sociologist Charles Horton Cooley coined the term "the looking-glass self."

Most intimately of all, our very consciousness is social. We think in words, but we did not invent them. We could not think at all if we did not have ideas, and we guide our behavior by certain ideals. But neither ideas nor ideals could have been created by ourselves alone. Ideas and ideals must have something *general* in them; they are concepts that transcend the particular and that make out each particular thing to be an example of a larger class of things. But nature always presents itself to us as particulars, never as generalities. Observing nature could never have suggested general concepts to us. Each tree is actually unique; it is only because we have the *general idea* of "tree" that we can see the resemblance among trees and thus treat them as members of the same class of things.

The only way we can transcend the here-and-now of *this* particular thing at *this* particular place is to put ourselves on another vantage point, one that cuts across time and space. But this is what society does. Hence whenever we think, we do so by means of concepts that originated in social communication. Communication must always jump above any one person's particular viewpoint to a bridge of generality connecting one person's reality with another's. Social communication is what creates our basic repertoire of ideas, insofar as ideas are abstract concepts. Since we use these ideas to think with, our own minds are permeated by society. We cannot escape society, even when we are alone. As long as we are conscious, society is implicitly there.

Thus society is both outside us and within the very core of our consciousness. This is what makes the symbolism of religion so very powerful: it expresses the essential facts of our human existence. That is why religious symbolism has incorporated ideas of human identity as well as of social obligation, why there is the idea of a soul as well as of some kind of god or spiritual force that rules the universe. And since religion symbolizes the major facts of society, it has always had to make room for social conflict in its system of symbols. Since societies are never totally unified, religion must always describe the existence of rival gods, heretics, evil spirits, or the devil. The symbolism of religion mirrors the social world.

WHY DO PEOPLE HAVE MORAL FEELINGS?

But religion is more than an intellectual reality. Above all, it is a moral force. This, too, is preeminently social. Notions of right and wrong are intrinsically collective. Most of them regulate the relationships among people: prohibitions against killing, lying, and stealing, or positive injunctions to love or aid your neighbor. None of these rules make sense except in a social context. Even those moral rules that do not refer explicitly to social behavior have an underlying social component. Respect for a ritual is right, and a violation of it is wrong, because the group decrees it so. It is offensive to a believer for someone to spit on the Bible, for example, but only because the group has made the Bible into a sacred object.

The very idea of morality implies a force beyond any particular individual, a force that makes demands and punishes transgressions. These demands and punishments are not ordinary ones. You are expected to follow a moral duty, regardless of whether it is useful or injurious to yourself. Utilitarian rewards and punishments on the mundane plane, in the profane world, are irrelevant to whether something is right or wrong. If you believe that stealing is wrong, then it is wrong even if you were to gain a great deal by stealing; it would continue to be wrong even if you were never caught. The punishment for a moral transgression, rather, is in another realm, just as the reward for moral behavior is in Heaven or in whatever the sacred realm is considered to be in that society.

What is the reality of Heaven and Hell and their equivalents in other religions? The only real force that can fill their part is society itself. Moral righteousness is what makes you a member in good standing of the group; the secure sense of belonging constitutes its reward. This is what Heaven symbolizes. Moral evil is a transgression against the group, and its punishment on the strictly moral plane is automatic: it is the exclusion from membership. In the symbolism of Christian theology, Hell is the banishment of the sinner from God. Moral punishment is to be excluded from the feeling of belonging to society.

Why do people adhere to the precepts of morality? First of all, because the group demands it. But also because individuals want to belong. It is hard for people to avoid having some moral feelings or other because almost everyone is attached to some social group. Insofar as they want to belong to the group, they automatically attach themselves to its morality. It is social ties that produce these spontaneous feelings of what are considered right and wrong.

This does not necessarily mean that everyone shares the same morality, or that everyone has equally intense moral feelings. On the contrary. If morality comes from group membership, then the fact that there are different sorts of groups in a society, that groups are in conflict with one another, and that individuals may join or leave groups means that there will be a number of different moralities. Which group one wishes to belong to will determine what kind of moral feelings they will have. If groups are in conflict, then their moralities will be in conflict too. This is true in the secular realm as well as in the sphere of religion. People who belong to opposing political parties regard their own position as right, and their opponents' policies as wrong, in much the same fashion as members of rival religions feel themselves to be righteous and the others to be sinners.

Whatever the group may be, though, if people want to belong to it they will end up feeling some kind of moral obligation. This sounds like the individual has to sacrifice something to become a member. The sacrifice is real enough, but there are compensations.

One of the main benefits of belonging to a group is so close to home that it tends to be overlooked. It is intangible, but completely real. This is the emotional energy that one receives from taking part in intense social gatherings. It is because of this emotional energy that people can do things in crowds that they cannot or would not do alone. The crowd makes them feel strong because they are part of some thing that is much stronger than they are as individuals. It also tends to make them feel righteous because by participating in a common activity they are doing something more than merely acting on their own individual self-interest. It is for these reasons that people acting together in groups are capable of much stronger exertions than they usually would be alone.

We see this in a very common form at athletic events. The individual athlete is spurred on by a large and sympathetic crowd, and athletes performing as part of a close-knit team can sometimes perform beyond limits they would ordinarily find impossible. The same kind of sentiments are played upon in very dangerous situations like military battles. Ordinarily people's level of courage is not very high, especially when they are by themselves. But in warfare troops have frequently stood together under very heavy fire and accepted almost certain death; the courage lasts as long as the group keeps together and feels that everyone is facing the same danger.

The energy and moral force of an assembled group is thus both very powerful and potentially very dangerous. It is these group situations that bring individuals to the highest levels of altruism. They become capable of heroic actions and personal self-sacrifice. Individuals are capable of becoming martyrs, especially if it can be done in public and with a strong supporting cast. At the same time, a crowd easily loses all sense of restraint. The moral energy can quickly become fanatical and can be turned in many different directions. From the excitement of mass gatherings, crusades are born and revolutions are made. Smaller groups are usually less excitable, but they too have an effect of picking up the energy level of the people who throw themselves into them.

So one very powerful way to gain confidence and energy is to participate in intense group situations. Politics and religion have a common root. Religious leaders or political orators, in particular, tend to gain a high degree of personal energy from their social role. The leader who can focus the attention of the crowd, who can express an idea that the audience holds in common, becomes filled with special energies. If the group is excited enough, the group leader becomes inspired, more than just an ordinary person. He or she can become charismatic, a celebrity, a hero, even a holy figure. The energy that produces this transformation does not come from the leader. It is the energy of the group, revved up by passing around the assembled crowd, and brought to a focus by the leader who speaks to them and for them. The leader is the channel for the collective energy, and that is what seems to exalt him or her above the individuals in the mass. But the secret of the leader's power is the group itself. It is the audience that creates the prophet; it is the movement that creates the leader.

The leader reaps the greatest rewards from participating in the group. The political leader, speaking for the group's ideals, becomes its most energetic member. The priest saying mass is the holiest person in the church because he is the center of the ceremony that everyone else watches. But ordinary rank-and-file group members can receive an emotional benefit too. They do not get quite the same energy surge, the same feeling of righteousness, as the leader, but they do gain personal force and confidence from participating in group gatherings. The more enthusiastically they throw themselves into the spirit of the meeting, the more of a sense of exaltation they receive. By participating in their church, their political rally, or whatever group they may attach themselves to, they gain an increment of energy and self-confidence that makes them feel capable of achieving things they could not otherwise reach.

Group meetings, then, are a kind of social machine for transforming energies. By plugging into the group situation, individuals can make themselves stronger and more purposeful. This is the hidden payoff that accounts for the continuous appeal of religion and its secular equivalents.

The duality of the sacred and the profane, that basic distinction that makes up the content of all religious beliefs, corresponds to an alternation between two modes of social organization. Much of the time society is dispersed; people pursue their mundane tasks, making a living, eating, consuming, following their own practical interests and concerns. The level of collective energy is low, as people have only their own resources to draw upon. But alternating with these times of dispersion are times of assembly. These are the archetypal religious situations. It may be the meeting of a church or the celebration of a tribal rite. In either case, the gathering of the society changes the energy dynamics. The mood of the Australian clan coming together, for example, is a concentration and mutual stimulation that passes among the assembled members like an electric charge. Common emotions are built up. The world of everyday profane tasks is replaced by another mood, one that is more intense and directed toward a different aim. By means of its symbols, the group no longer focuses upon the individual tasks of the mundane world but upon its collective self. It is out of this that people derive the sense of a higher realm, which they call the divine. It is a realm of the spirit, precisely because it is a spirit within which the group participates.

A GENERAL MODEL OF SOCIAL RITUALS

If we look at the elements that go into producing a religious feeling, we arrive at a general model of social rituals. As indicated, this can be looked at as the formula for a machine for transforming social energies and also a machine for creating social ideals or symbols.

What are the components of this machine?

First of all, *the group must be assembled.* It is the physical presence of other people that starts the energies flowing, building up the contagious emotion.

But this by itself is not enough. The individuals in the group must all come to feel the same emotion and become conscious that the others are sharing it. Thus *actions must be ritualized.* People must carry out a pattern, coordinating their gestures and voices. This may be done in unison or by means of a script in which each person plays their expected part. Ritualized actions are regular and rhythmic, whether in the extreme form of singing, chanting, or dancing together, or in the more loose-knit form of an audience applauding the words of a leader. It is the common action that enables the group to feel itself as a group. It is no longer a static collection of individuals, but a dynamic, mutually coherent force.

Finally there is an emblem or *symbolic object that focuses the group's idea of itself.* The power of the group is its energy and its moral force, but this is hard for people to understand directly. Participating in it themselves, people cannot see it for what it is. They must represent its reality under a concrete form. They *reify* it: they come to believe it is a real, almost physical, thing. Thus they conceive of the spirit that moves and unites them as a sacred object. It is the totem animal in whose name they assemble, or the God to whom they pray. In the modern political version, it is the nation, the party, or the political idea (e.g., democracy, or socialism, or revolution), which they feel they are fighting for.

The underlying reality of any symbol is the group itself, and more particularly the mood its members feel when they assemble and carry out their rituals. This sense of group identity becomes attached to an idea, which is simultaneously an ideal—a perfect or divine entity to which individuals must subordinate themselves, in return for which they receive security and emotional strength.

The emotion attached to this idea is diffuse and contagious. It has the quality of transcending ordinary reality so that its essence cannot be completely grasped. It also has the quality of spreading out and adhering to specific, concrete objects. Not only is the mythical totem or the almighty God divine, but so also is the carved wooden emblem that represents the totem, or the altar or the cross by which God is worshipped. Thus there are not only sacred ideas, but sacred objects, which must be treated with respect.

The existence of sacred things gives religions yet another dimension. Since they are concrete and material, such objects give a feeling of permanence. The spirit of the group lives on in them, even when the group is not assembled. True enough, the feeling of exaltation and emotional strength that comes from the group could not survive if the group did not reassemble before too much time elapses. The emotion-producing machine has to be run intermittently since its charges run down in between times. But concrete symbols can act as batteries, storing up the social energy, and reminding the faithful members of that in which they believe and the feeling that it represents.

The symbols also can be used to reassemble the group, to crank up the machine again. Once charged with emotional significance, a sacred emblem can be used as a focal point around which another performance of the ritual can be carried out. Thus concrete emblems carry over at least a minimal feeling of solidarity from one ritual celebration to another. It is upon the ongoing existence of such emblems that the continuity of the group's identity depends.

The same principle applies to words as to physical objects. If a cross or a flag can be a concrete symbol of the group, a particular name or statement of belief can serve equally well. Thus the names of gods have always been sacred for their believers and so have the particular doctrines that believers hold about their religion. Just as in the case of physical emblems, these verbal symbols serve to reinvoke a feeling of membership when one is alone and to reassemble the group for new devotions. Particular names and doctrines take on emotional charges from the rituals in which they originate, and hence serve as the basis of social memory and as a rallying point for putting on a new performance of the ritual. Since words can be carried around in people's heads, the fact that they can serve as sacred symbols gives a great deal of flexibility to the "machinery" of social membership. Even without physical emblems, people can reinvoke feelings of group solidarity just by remembering certain phrases or calling a particular name—Allah, Jesus, or whatever it may be. If they do this together with other people, their very conversation becomes transformed into an impromptu social ritual.

This last point is particularly important because it gives people a clue about how to act toward one another. On the one hand, if two people both respect the same sacred emblems and the same holy names, and share the same doctrines, they know that they belong to the same ritual community. They can identify with one another as members of a group that has feelings of collective solidarity and strength. To put it differently, they both know how to act as parts of a particular emotion-transforming machine that lifts them to a higher level of security and energy. And in their own encounters, even in a short conversation, they can carry out a miniature ritual that gives an immediate emotional payoff. It also gives them a particular identity, a way of defining themselves. In tribal Australia those who worship the same totem share a common name. All those who call themselves after the kangaroo, for example, regard themselves as related, and feel bound to aid and not to hurt one another, just as they are bound not to kill the kangaroo. In Christianity or Islam, co-religionists call themselves by the name of their sect and feel they are brethren in the faith. They identify with each other's triumph and troubles, and feel obligated to come to one another's aid. The same bonds of common identity and moral solidarity are found among the adherents of any other strong religious or political doctrine.

But the same principle works in a negative sense, too. Sacred symbols enable people to identify those whom they cannot trust. For if the existence of sacred symbols indicates a common identity and moral ties among those who worship in the same cult, encountering someone who does not recognize these same sacred objects indicates a boundary between groups. At the least, those who do not share the same symbols feel a lack of positive emotional ties; they are strangers, mutual outsiders.

These feelings can easily develop from mere neutrality into outright hostility. In fact, it is the existence of sacred objects that creates the opportunity for hostility. A ritual cult creates a sense of belonging and a shared morality that would not be there without the cult; any actions that violate the ritual or its sacred objects threaten the sense of group security. Hence it calls forth an angry response. For someone to desecrate a holy place, to burn a Bible or a totem emblem or a flag, to curse a holy name or utter a remark of political disloyalty, is to challenge the group that organizes itself around that symbol. The same is true for disagreeing with a doctrine that the group takes as a matter of common faith: it constitutes social heresy.

It is not surprising that any group that is strong enough will severely punish the perpetrator of such symbolic offenses. It makes no difference that little or no real physical harm may be done by the offender. The violator has challenged something far more emotion-laden than a piece of mundane property; hence the reaction is not just an effort at restitution but a feeling of righteous outrage. Notice the *righteous* aspect of this reaction: it is precisely because the group ritual creates feelings of morality that group punishments of ritual violations have this tone of *moral* anger. In terms of the metaphor used above, whoever tampers with the social-energy transforming machine runs the danger of receiving a high-intensity shock.

We find in a theory of religion, then, explanations of a wide range of phenomena. It shows us that life involves two quite different sorts of experiences, those in which individuals are reminded of their dependence upon the group and those in which they pursue their own practical interests. It is from the former type of experience that we derive our general ideas and ideals, and our feelings of morality. A theory of religion is also a theory of rituals and symbols: rituals being the coordinated actions of an assembled group that gives its members a special emotional energy; symbols being ideas, emblems, and doctrines that represent the group experience. Symbols are felt to be sacred by those who use them to constitute their group; hence people who share common symbols feel a moral tie among themselves and a righteous anger against outsiders who violate the respect they feel is due to their symbols.

We have, then, an explanation of what holds groups together and of what keeps them apart. We have an explanation of ideas, and of morality in both its positive and negative aspects. And all of this follows the injunction of the preceding chapter, to show the nonrational foundations of rationality.

There are many ways in which this theory can be applied. We have already seen that the theory extends beyond religion proper: there are political rituals and ideas—we may call them ideologies—as well as religious ones. There is a good deal more to politics, of course, than the ritual aspects of assembled crowds; an explanatory theory of politics must also deal with interests and resources, with power and conflict. Later chapters of this book will touch upon these issues again, showing where rituals fit in with property and force. Another possibility would be to take up the theme of ritual violations and the righteous anger they provoke, which leads to a theory of crime and punishment. This, too, is reserved for a later chapter.

For now, let us stick close to the phenomenon of religion. Examining it from the point of view of its variations and its historical changes, brings us even more evidence that religion is a social phenomenon. And by a strange evolution, it brings us to see our modern, secular society as full of rituals that carry on the older religious forces in a new guise. In some of the most common activities of everyday life, we find religion gone underground.

THE TYPE OF GOD CORRESPONDS TO THE TYPE OF SOCIETY

If God represents society, then it should follow that different types of societies should have different types of gods. There should be a correspondence between the type of religion and the structure of the social group. As the societies change, the religions should change as well.

As it happens, this is precisely what we find when we compare different religions.

In tribal societies, there is a close connection between the religion and the social structure. Hunting-and-gathering societies, like those Durkheim described in Australia, are small groups, rarely exceeding a few hundred people when fully assembled. They have virtually no wealth and no hierarchy. All the different clans that make up the tribe are equal, as are, by and large, the people within them. Their religion shows the same kind of structure. Corresponding to each clan, there is a sacred totem (the black cockatoo, the white cockatoo, the kangaroo, etc.) that gives the clan its name and is the center of its special rites and beliefs. All totems are religiously equal. Each is special for its own group; none stands out over the others. This horizontal multiplicity of sacred objects corresponds to the horizontal organization of the tribe.

The only stratification found within Australian societies is that by age and sex. The older men dominate the women and the younger men. This feature, too, shows up in the religion. The women are excluded entirely from religious ceremonies and are not allowed even to see the sacred emblems. The young males are eventually allowed into the religious cult, but only by passing through painful initiation rites.

When we move on to tribal societies that practice crude agriculture (horticulture), we find that both the religion and the social structure have changed. Such societies are larger, more settled, and have some accumulated wealth. They are usually structured around elaborate kinship systems. There are complex rules as to who should marry whom; which marriages are prohibited; with whose family the bride, groom, and children should live; and what goods must be paid between the inter-marrying families. In such societies, the role of women tends to be quite important. Many of these tribes are matrilineal (the children inherit their name and their property from their mothers' line) or matrilocal (husbands go to live, at least part of the time, with their wives' family). Women are also central to the economy, doing most of the agricultural work, as well as crafts such as weaving and pottery-making. Thus women produce most of the property.

It should not come as a surprise, in this case, that the religions of such societies tend to have a heavily female emphasis. The main cults often center on fertility rites, which symbolically equate sexual intercourse and child-bearing with planting and harvesting crops. Women take an important part in religious ceremonies. The sacred doctrines frequently concern mythical females, and the sacred emblems of the religion often represent women with exaggerated breasts and genitals. Men, however, are not exactly subordinated in these societies, and play an important role especially in politics and war. These religions have male as well as female components. But it is a striking illustration of the Durkheimian theory that the type of societies in which women are most prominent should also be those in which the religions are the most female-oriented.

The more productive the economy becomes in agricultural societies, the more scope there is for large-scale social organization. Quite a variety of social types and intermixtures becomes possible. Particular groups may specialize in animal herding, fishing, or trade; towns and cities appear; armies are organized. If we look at all of these societies as a whole, we notice another religious pattern. We now can see a range of political organizations, from religiously independent, egalitarian groups up through local chiefdoms, military coalitions, and kingdoms united under a powerful throne. Parallel with this variety of political organization is a corresponding set of religions.

Generally speaking, the more levels of political organization in a society, the more hierarchy there is within the realm of religion. If there is a multitiered political structure with aristocrats and officials at the top, dominating a lower rank on down to a bottom rung of peasants and slaves, the gods are likely to be thought of as arranged in a hierarchy as well, with full-fledged gods and goddesses at the top, minor spirits at the bottom. The more centralized the political organization, the more levels of hierarchy under an all-powerful king, the more likely the religion is to conceive of a high god presiding over all the rest, like the Greeks' Zeus presiding over Mt. Olympus. As states conquer one another, the gods of the defeated states are often incorporated into the pantheon; they become lower religious forces subordinate to the god who represents the conquering state. Such gods are usually represented as heavenly warriors, all-powerful masculine figures, a king of kings in the sky reflecting the king of kings upon the earth. Religion here not only reflects society but acts as part of the apparatus of domination, serving to make the upper class appear especially powerful and awe-inspiring.

One more form of religion appears along with the rise of literate, cosmopolitan civilizations. In periods like the ancient

Roman Empire, or contemporaneous periods in India, China, and Persia, the idea emerged that all the different names for the gods represent a single transcendent reality. The pantheons are reduced to a single God or a single mystical condition. Christianity, Buddhism, Hindu mysticism, Taoism, Confucianism, Zoroastrianism, and later Islam—these are called the "world religions" because each one sees a single spiritual force in the entire world. Each declares that there is but a single God, a single state of Enlightenment, or a single Way; all other gods are false or illusory.

This type of religion, in short, aims to be universal. It corresponds to a rationalized, literate society, one with such great political power that it can foster the idea of a universal state spanning the whole known world.

Looking back over the entire range of societies, from hunting-and-gathering tribes to the great world empires, we can see that the type of gods conceived of in each corresponds to the size and structure of the society. God represents society, not only in a general sense, but in detail. Each particular type of society has its own particular type of god.

A historical question then arises. What changes first, the religion or the society? Does religion cause social change or vice versa? No one has attempted to prove the case one way or the other for all the types of societies we have reviewed above. But an argument has been made about one particular transition from one type to another. Max Weber, writing at about the same time as Durkheim, proposed that the rise of modern capitalist, industrial society, was due to a change in the sphere of religion. In his early writings he attributes this to the rise of a particular form of Protestantism; in other writings, he describes the whole political and economic development of the modern world as growing out of the distinctive forms of Christianity and ancient Judaism.

Other sociologists have reversed the causal hypothesis. Marxists argue that religions are ideologies arising from the social structure that reinforce the domination by the ruling class and the form of property upon which it is built. Yet a third position is taken by structuralists, such as Claude Lévi-Strauss. For them, the structure of the society and the structure of the religion (or of ideas and myths generally) make up a whole. They do not ask which comes first or which causes which, but concentrate instead on describing the basic elements within these structures out of which the whole is constructed.

I shall not pursue this issue any further here. Its ramifications make up one of the key questions still being asked in sociology today, and throughout the social sciences and the sciences of culture.

THE RISE OF THE INDIVIDUAL SELF

The sociological theory of religion has been applied not only to the macrolevel questions of the structure of entire societies and their historical changes; it has also given rise to a good deal of microanalysis. This concerns relatively small groups and brief interactions—in short, the rituals and symbols of everyday life.

It may seem strange, in the light of the preceding argument, that any microlevel rituals would still exist in large-scale modern societies. If God represents society, then as society gets larger, God becomes increasingly greater and more remote. Moreover, as Durkheim himself pointed out, as societies become more complex, the idea of God must become more abstract. With a complex social division of labor, individual members of society have more specialized life experiences and become increasingly different from one another. Hence any symbol that represents all of society must have less and less specific content. God moves away from being conceived as a concrete emblem, like the Australian totem, and even beyond being conceived as a person, like one of the Greek gods or goddesses. In the great world religions, God or Ultimate Reality is declared to be beyond all worldly characterization and, thus, can only be described negatively or in abstract superlatives—as unbounded, infinite, unending, omniscient, supremely good. It becomes blasphemy to see God as limited to being merely a kind of super-person.

There is even a further step in this development. As God becomes sufficiently abstract, eventually all the anthropomorphic elements disappear. In industrial societies, Durkheim argued, the scope of the division of labor becomes so great that even the very general idea of God tends to disappear into the air. It turns into a general conception of humanity. The moral boundaries of religion have been increasing with every transition to a more inclusive conception of God. Where the tribal religion sanctified moral actions among fellow members of the tribe but left members of other tribes as outsiders, the increasing scope of religious ideals successively widened the range of people toward whom a believer must act morally. At first, one is only prohibited from killing or stealing from fellow members of the totemic group; eventually, one is not supposed to kill or steal from anyone. With the idea of a universal religion, came the moral ideas of a family of humanity comprising the entire world.

As it happened, none of the great world religions quite lived up to its promise. Christianity, and within it, its various sects, Islam and its sects, the different forms of Buddhism, and so forth, each tended to become identified with particular states or social groups, and to carry on persecutions and wars against one another. With the rise of the cosmopolitan societies of modern times, a reaction set in against this moral chauvinism. Enlightened people of the eighteenth and nineteenth centuries came to disbelieve any of the particular doctrines and symbols of the warring religions, and to put in their place a conception of morality that transcended all doctrinal prejudices. The very idea of the supernatural began to disappear. But its fundamental content lived on. For if the basic symbolism of religion represents society, then this content can be found in doctrines that focus on the good of humanity and on schemes to preserve or improve society. Religion, pushed to the extreme generalization and abstraction, turns into political ideals. Thus modern political doctrines, such as conservatism, liberalism, and socialism, emerge out of the declining belief in religion. They also continue its concerns in a new form.

We are still talking about the macrolevel of whole societies and the doctrines that aim at serving them. But by an interesting twist, this development of religion into more and more abstract forms, and finally into political ideologies, has a counterpart on the microlevel. As societies have gotten larger and more complex, individuals within them have grown increasingly distinctive from one another. In a tribal society, in which virtually everyone does the same thing as everyone else, individual personalities tend to resemble each other. In a complex industrial society, we are close to the opposite extreme. Each individual personality tends to live in their own specialized world. Thus the same social changes that make religion more remote and abstract, also make people more individualistic.

INTERACTION RITUALS IN EVERYDAY LIFE

One of the followers of Durkheim's school of thought, Erving Goffman, has tied the two processes together rather neatly. The religious rituals and beliefs that represent the whole society have become so general and remote in the modern world as to virtually disappear from everyday life. The ceremonies, prayers, saying grace, and so forth, that used to mark almost every hour of the day have gone. In their place have appeared rituals that are so common as to be taken for granted. Goffman calls these *interaction rituals*.

Interaction rituals take place in ordinary conversation. The ritual often takes the form of what we ordinarily think of as politeness. The ideal or sacred object that is attached to it is the individual *self*.

What can this mean?

It means, first of all, that one's self is not the same as one's body. The body is part of the physical world, the self part of the social. Our name, our self-image, our consciousness—all of these, as Durkheim has already described, come from our interactions

with other people. Your self is an *idea* that you hold, and an idea
that other people hold about you, too.

This implies that people under different sorts of social interactions acquire different kinds of selves. Corresponding to the
comparison we have just run through of different sorts of societies and their religions, we could make a comparison of the
particular kinds of selves that people have in each of these societies. Generally speaking, we would find that the conception
of the self shifts across this continuum from being highly embedded in the group to being individualistic.

In a tribal society, for example, individuals conceive of themselves as part of the clan. Whatever special skills or energies
they have are usually attributed to outside forces such as magic
or the power of the totem. These spiritual forces are ways of
representing a strong feeling of social influences pressing upon
the person from outside. In more complex agrarian societies,
these all-encompassing religious forces have retreated a bit, although unusual things that people do are still explained by the
intervention of God, Fate, or some other spiritual force. In these
societies, as well, there continue to be strong social pressures
upon each individual. People tend to be extremely dependent
upon their families and tied into rigid social rankings. There is
little privacy; people live in conditions in which everyone's life
is open to continuous inspection by those around them. Not sur-
prisingly, there is only a limited conception of the individual
self. People are expected to be completely loyal to their families
and their superiors. They are given little choice in whom they
should marry or where they should work. The legal system gives
little consideration to persons; an entire family or village could
be held responsible for the crimes of one of its members, and
violent punishments such as tortures and mutilations are considered entirely acceptable. People are not supposed to have
individual opinions, and conformity to prevailing doctrines is
rigidly enforced. Individual conscience does not matter; what
counts is external conformity to the group.

Modern urban society, then, can be considered unusual for

its conception of each individual as having an inner self. In the law, individuals are now held responsible for their own actions, and the degree of guilt or innocence comes to hinge on questions of subjective intention. Did someone knowingly and deliberately commit such and such an act? That is what decides court cases today. This criterion shows both that people are now conceived of as having subjective selves, capable of thinking and deciding—a conception that most earlier societies lacked—and furthermore, that people are *required* to act according to such an individually responsible self. The notion of the inner, individual self is not only a prevailing image in the world today, but it is an ideal that today's morality demands that each of us have.

This should alert us to the way in which modern individualism is itself a kind of religious cult. We are not only allowed to be individuals, we are *expected* to be. Society does not give us a choice in the matter.

How is this sense of individual, inner consciousness produced then? We should expect that it is produced in the same way that any other moral ideals are produced, by a particular kind of ritual. This is the ritual that Goffman finds us following in our everyday encounters.

Conversations today, by and large, are carried out casually and informally. There seems to be little of the rigid ceremony that would remind us of old-fashioned rituals. But it is the very casualness that makes them appropriate as rituals commemorating the individual self.

We continually emphasize that we are giving our own opinions, not acting out some external role. Joking and irony are very popular ways of speaking today; these are ways of demonstrating that we can maintain a psychological detachment from the pressures and social organizations around us. Complaining and criticizing, other very popular conversational activities, are yet more ways of keeping ourselves independent. Goffman describes how these modes of acting out one's self can build up into friendly or unfriendly contests, where people try to "one-up" each other by joking at each other's expense and outdoing each other in irony. All this constitutes a kind of cult of the ultra-self, demonstrating that you can produce endless layers of inner detachment from everything that other people can throw at you.

However, the main forms of self-creating interaction rituals are not competitive but cooperative. People cooperate in building up each other's self-image. Much of conversation involves what might be called "white lies." People exaggerate, building up incidents in their daily lives to be more exciting than they really are, pretending to be smarter or cooler or richer or more successful than is actually the case, painting their adversaries in darker colors than fit the facts. By and large conversationalists get away with these exaggerations. It even seems to be expected of them. Each individual seems to give the other the tacit right to build up a somewhat false view of their own world in return for the right to do likewise when it is their turn to speak.

All this, trivial as it may be in any particular conversation, adds up to maintaining each person's inner self. For the idea of oneself, like all "sacred" ideals, needs to be continuously reinforced from outside. Conversation is a series of little rituals in which the cult of the ego is maintained. It is a peculiarly social egotism because each individual depends upon their friends to validate their own egotistical world view. As Goffman puts it, social interaction is a circular process in which everyone gives another an ideal self and receives back in return their own self from other people.

Goffman goes a good deal further into the methods by which social selves are created. He compares social life to a theater in which there are frontstages and backstages. On the "frontstage," people put on an idealized picture of themselves, wearing the proper clothes, making the right facial expressions, and using the right words and gestures. In the "backstage," people prepare their roles beforehand, and then afterwards relax and recover from the efforts of being "onstage." There are many different sorts of frontstages and backstages: political, occupational, commercial, social. One may even conceive of backstages behind backstages, as one moves to successively more intimate settings. Psychotherapy, or extremely personal conversations, are some of the extreme backstages of today, where things that cannot be revealed on other backstages become the objects of attention.

A modern self, then, can become quite complicated. Goffman shows that there can be quite a variety of layers within layers, different forms of socially shared pretenses each of which takes a certain amount of social effort to be carried off successfully. In one of his later metaphors, he describes this as being like a set of picture frames, where another frame can always be put around the frames that already exist.

The question naturally arises: is there a final self behind all these layers? It might seem that if we go on stripping away all these different kinds of performances, we might arrive at the kernel of individual consciousness, the puppeteer who pulls the strings of all the puppets. But Goffman does not think so. None of the types of social self he describes can be created without cooperative social interaction. In fact, we each can have all these inner laminations only because of the complicated social world we now inhabit. *It is because we can move among a variety of group situations, and because we are encouraged to present an ideal self in each one, that all this inner complexity emerges.*

In short, we could presumably go on adding an infinite number of inner layers, without ever reaching the center. The layers are added from the outside, which then get reflected on the inside in our consciousness. Each new level of individual is created by a new way of relating to other people. There is no pre-social self. The lonely, individual self has only come into existence with a complex form of society.

This conclusion should not be surprising. After all, we have seen that religion is created by society and that individualism is the distinctively modern form that religion takes. It is the structure of modern society that allows us the "backstage" of privacy that other societies lacked and that creates the possibility of idealizing our behavior toward some people when we converse with them. The idea of the individual with a unique, inner self is one that emerges from these distinctively modern patterns of interaction.

Like any other sacred object created by social rituals, the modern self is something of a myth. It is nowhere near as autonomous and individualistic as it makes itself out to be. Again, this is not surprising for beneath every mythical symbol, there is the same reality: society. If society now symbolizes itself in the idea of the subjective self, it is because this is the one thing that a complex division of labor still allows us to have in common.

THE WORLD OF SOCIAL RITUALS

The theory of social rituals, then, may be based on religion, but it expands far into every corner of social life. This becomes clear when we recall the fundamental point that social groups of any type are not based simply upon rational choice but upon subrational feelings of solidarity. Small, isolated, and homogeneous groups put a very strong pressure upon the individual, and this is what generates the feelings expressed in religious beliefs about the omnipresence of supernatural spirits. For those individuals in modern society whose social experiences consist of a great variety of different encounters in the large-scale networks of acquaintanceship, the rituals of interaction take quite a different form. They remain rituals, nevertheless, and produce a distinctively modern type of "secular religion," the cult of individualism. Yet the cult of the individual is not the same thing as the completely isolated, self-directed person imagined by the commonsense idea of the rational choice-maker. As Goffman points out, one is not only allowed to be an individual, one is actually required to be so. When our social interactions take this form, we can't avoid having legal responsibility thrust upon us. And the same social conditions also produce the expectation that we should be self-aware, ironic, detached, and all the rest of the modern style of presenting the self. The modern ideal of the casual, "cool," self-possessed individual is not a reaction against society; it is the very form that social ideals are molded in today.

It is also true, though, that even in today's society we are not totally exposed to a shifting marketplace of relationships. We are not always faced with a kaleidescopic variety of different people and different social situations. Some of our experiences—during our childhood years, say, or perhaps inside certain tightly knit groups and organizations—are more like those high-density experiences that Durkheim described as the basis of primitive religion. Modern society is all manner of things, and along with the busy social marketplace that produces individualism there are also little modern "tribes." It is precisely in these places—in small towns or in the experiences of children confined to the same home, school, and neighborhood—that we continue to find little tribal rites of solidarity. The corresponding beliefs may take the form of revivals of traditional religions, or they may be modern cults like those of athletic teams or school fraternities. There are political, occupational, and intellectual cults as well, which generate strong emotional commitments and support symbolic beliefs sacred to each particular group. All these operate quite strongly in the modern scene as long as the group manages to keep assembling and carrying out its own rituals.

As we have seen, rituals are a kind of social technology that can be put to a variety of uses. The machine can be adjusted to various settings, so that the same mechanism can produce many different outcomes. On one setting—the high-density end of the spectrum—we get the rather fanatical and superstitious beliefs of primitive tribes. At another setting, the result is Goffman's world of ironic individualism. Still other pulls on the social levers result in the ideological sentiments of mass politics or the intensity of social movements. There are rituals of harmony as well as those of conflict. Sometimes people consciously manipulate rituals to bolster their own domination over others. At other times rituals arise spontaneously because of the way people happen to be thrown together in face-to-face situations.

The theory of rituals can take us a long way through the varieties of social life. In succeeding chapters, I will make use of it, together with some other nonobvious ideas of sociology.

3

PARADOXES OF POWER

Power is one of those words that seems to have an obvious and straightforward meaning. Someone is described as a powerful political leader; so-and-so is the real power in the business community; some people are so powerful that you can't possibly risk offending them. Institutions, too, are described as powerful: someone holds the powerful position of secretary of an important union; this or that committee is powerful in an organization. And, of course, all official positions carry certain powers with them.

Nevertheless, when we probe beneath the surface of what we believe about power, the pattern becomes a good deal less obvious. People who are reputed to be powerful do not necessarily get their way. Very often officials are restricted in all sorts of ways that gives them very little room to exercise their authority. Political leaders are notorious for making promises to carry out a program and then ending up unable to do it. Even those whose power seems most absolute—the top executive of a corporation or the head of a dictatorial government—do not always get their way. A tycoon may order his secretary around, but he can't necessarily keep the corporation from going bankrupt; and even the bloodiest of dictators are sometimes overthrown by a revolution or *coup*.

Power over human beings is not quite the same thing as power over the inanimate world. Social power is not the same thing as electric power; you cannot merely push a button and be sure the lights will go on.

As we examine it, the nature of power becomes much more subtle than at first glance. We can see this by looking at both when it actually works and when it fails to work. The successful power wielder is not just pressing buttons; he or she is engaging in some quite complex social manipulation. Individuals who manage to be powerful and get their own way must do so by going along with the laws of social organization, not by contradicting them. There is no such thing as a social superman, impervious to bullets and travelling faster than the speed of light. The powerful individual is one who goes with the grain of things, who acquires what power the social organization at that time has to offer.

Those who want to make something happen in society are engaged in an exercise of power. They are attempting to impose their will on others. They may have an official right to do this, if they are an elected office-holder, the owner of a company, the teacher of a class, or the like. Nevertheless, it is not so easy to get a policy carried out. The use of power always sets in motion countercurrents. People below the top ranks implicitly resist any too overbearing exercise of power. They go along enthusiastically only to the extent that they agree with what is being done. And even then disagreements are common over how things are to be carried out and who gets to carry the ball. Power generates conflicts, even in the best of circumstances. These conflicts are most obvious in the realm of politics, but any kind of organization where some people control others has an undercurrent of struggle over how things will be done.

One of the most common forms of struggle is economic. It takes place in any organization where people hold jobs in order to make a living. People do not necessarily think of themselves in Marxian terms as part of a conflict of worker versus bourgeoisie, but economic issues come up over and over again just the same. Sometimes the issue comes out in the form of workers going on strike. At other times it is a struggle of individuals pursuing their economic self-interest in the small daily issues of work. Every employee has constantly to decide just how hard to work, how much effort to put out, how much initiative to take on the job. How assiduously should orders be obeyed? Is it worth it to work as hard as possible? Does the pay match the effort? These sorts of issues are always implicitly present, and there is a subtle negotiation whenever an employer tries to get anyone to do anything.

Such economic issues, moreover, are only part of what the struggle is about. People want other things besides money—some power of their own, self-esteem in their job, a relatively pleasant work place, and a congenial set of people working around them. There are many things for people to contend over whenever someone tries to get them to do something.

This means that attempts to use power usually become embroiled in social conflicts. In these conflicts, the people with the most social resources usually win. But just what they win may not match up with what they set out to accomplish. What organizations actually do is a compromise among all the different contending interests within it. The same applies to the realm of politics and to the larger society in general. The outcomes are not so much what anyone in particular intended as they are the result of the sum total of conflicts that are going on.

One way to see what actually happens is to follow the different strategies that a leader, a manager, or an official could use in trying to exercise power over their subordinates. I have no particular bias toward the managers' side in this; it is only a convenient way of describing what happens. The same analysis tells us something about the counterstrategies available to the people who resist having power enforced upon them. Some controls work better than others in certain circumstances, but they all have their hidden drawbacks and unexpected consequences. First I examine three different ways of trying to exert control.

THREE STRATEGIES: MONEY, FORCE, AND SOLIDARITY

The most obvious way to get other people to do something is to pay them to do it. This assumes that you have the money to begin with. But assuming that you do, you can now set up your business, fund your government agency, found your school or whatever, and begin to exert power over the people on your payroll.

But though money may be power, it is not necessarily very effective power. The problem is you can pay people, but that does not in itself exert controls over just what they will do on the job. Supposing you pay them at the end of each month. The check comes automatically, whether they've done a good job or not. That isn't so farfetched: it is the way most government civil service employees, or the people who work in large bureaucracies anywhere, are paid. Here the boss's only control is to fire someone who is not working well, but that may be a complicated thing to do. If you have to go through a civil service hearing or a union grievance and other formalities, it may take months or years before a nonproductive worker is laid off. So money is not very much of a control.

The obvious answer then would be to pay over much shorter time periods. Instead of paying by the month, you could give out paychecks every week. This is in fact the way in which most manual workers are paid. There is more of an effort to tie the money to exactly how much work is done. Instead of paying a monthly or a yearly salary, the way higher-ranking white-collar jobs do, one pays a set rate for each hour worked. Now this narrows it down a good deal; people have to show up at least a certain number of hours to get paid for them. Still, what are these warm bodies going to be doing besides looking at the clock and waiting until it's time to go home? Just because people are physically present doesn't say anything about how hard they will be working and how much they are producing.

The closest way to control workers is to tie the pay directly to what they turn out. Factory workers, for example, may get so many cents for each piece of machinery they make. This seems like an unbeatable control. The manager has only to count how many pieces have been turned out that day and pay the workers for just how much they did, no more, no less. Unfortunately, there are a number of drawbacks.

For one thing, all this incentive system does is control how fast people work. It doesn't control the quality. This probably could be counted, too, but then the piece-rate would have to be raised to get workers to slow down and turn out better work. Moreover, the use of a financial incentive system becomes an important influence upon the way workers think of their job. The most important thing for the manager is obviously the monetary controls; this becomes the most important thing for the worker also. In the manager's eyes, all the workers want to do is make as much money as possible for as little effort as possible. The manager's very attitude encourages this. It then becomes a contest between manager and worker over just how much pay can be gotten for how much work.

Consider what a manager has to do to set the piece rate. He or she must decide how hard workers can reasonably be expected to work and set the pay scale accordingly. If you pay too much for each piece—say $1.00 per piece—then the workers know they have only to turn out, say, thirty pieces a day to earn $30.00. Once they reach that limit, or whatever they think is a good day's pay, they will slow down and more or less take the rest of the day off. So a manager who sets the piece rate too high will not get the maximal amount of work from the workers. On the other hand, suppose the piece rate is set very low—say 10¢ a piece. At that rate, even if workers work as hard as possible—say turning out one hundred pieces a day—they still make only $10.00. This isn't enough to live on, and the worker will rather go on strike or quit and look for a better paying job.

Obviously the best rate to pay to get maximal production is somewhere in the middle range. But exactly how to find this is a problem. The manager can come and observe what good workers can reasonably be expected to do in a hard day's work without killing themselves. Then management knows how many pieces to expect and can adjust the pay scale accordingly. The trouble is that the workers know what is going on too, and when the manager times one of them to set the standard rate, the worker is going to be prepared. What ensues is a little dramatic performance—the worker trying to look as hard-working and all-absorbed as possible, and yet turning out the job as slowly and deliberately as can be done. The fewer pieces per day the boss thinks is a reasonable rate, the easier it is for workers to meet the quota without having to push themselves too hard.

This situation is a paradigm for all the different ways in which managers might try to control workers by monetary incentives. The workers always try to manipulate the situation to turn out as little work for as high wages as possible, while the managers do the reverse. Generally speaking, the result is a kind of standoff. Usually, the more complicated the work, the more the workers win this kind of battle. Piece-rate payment only works at all when there are lots of simple, discrete operations that can easily be counted. If the job is at all complicated, the system can't be applied. This is the case whenever what one worker does depends on what someone else does, for example, when assembling a complicated piece of equipment, in which one worker can't start his or her part until other people have already finished theirs. If the others haven't gotten through with their segment of the operation yet, any given worker may be standing around with nothing to do, through no fault of their own. These kinds of situations are fairly common, and hence really tight monetary controls of the piece-rate sort are not so often found as some looser form such as paying by sheer number of hours present on the job.

Money, then, is not such a powerful way to control people as one might think. So why not try something else? If all methods were allowed, one might think rather cold-bloodedly that force might be a more effective sanction. Money may be something

that people bargain over, take a little more or a little less. But
no one wants to be physically hurt, and there is no more ultimate sanction than the threat of death. Compared to that all else
pales: who would dare to disobey orders if they could lose their
life for it?

Historically, the coercion strategy has certainly been popular
enough. In traditional agricultural societies, force was certainly
very widely used. It was the way knights kept peasants in line,
and everyone else too. In our own times, we have had the spec-
tacle of the Nazi and the Russian forced labor camps. In our
own prison system, prisoners are sometimes put to work smashing rock piles or stamping out license plates.

The experience of all these highly coercive organizations,
however, shows one main thing: forced labor is not very efficient. The Nazis and the Russians tried to run factories and
mines with their slave labor, but even extremely brutal coercion
could not make them produce at a rate that was even partially
as high as normal free labor would produce. Premodern agriculture, where coercion was also widely used, never reached anything like the level of productivity of modern farming, especially
farms run by the hands of the farmers who owned them.

Why should this be so? Well, it is easy to see that force has
certain drawbacks. No one likes being coerced, and anyone who
tries to force other people into doing something is going to have
a resentful labor force. B. F. Skinner, the behavioral psychologist, has attempted to show this experimentally—on pigeons, as
it turns out, rather than on people. You can teach a pigeon to do
all kinds of things, from pecking at a lever to learning how to
play ping-pong, by rewarding it with pecks of corn. You can also
try to teach a pigeon by using negative controls, i.e., by punishing it when it doesn't do what you want it to do. But even on
simple tasks, punishment is far less effective than reward. You
might think that a pigeon would be especially eager to learn to
press a lever if it turned off an electric current that was shocking
its toes. But this apparently is not what is foremost in the pigeon's priorities. The first thing it tries to do is get out of the

cage; it runs around wildly, getting fearful and angry (though Skinner himself would not put in it those words), and even tries to bite the hand of the psychologist. After many experiments Skinner proclaimed the principle that reward is a much more effective means of getting compliance than punishment.

In these respects, at least, people don't act so very differently than Skinner's pigeons. When someone coerces them, the first thing they do is get upset. They try to fight back if they can, and if they can't, they try to escape. Going ahead and complying with what is asked is a last resort to avoid the threat of punishment, but even then they do not work very willingly. Any boss who tries to coerce their labor force, then, has to be prepared to spend a lot of effort, and extra manpower, to keep workers from running away or rebelling. A slave-labor camp is different from a regular factory, in part, because it has a large number of guards who don't work but who have to be there to make sure anyone does any work at all.

Even if the security force is well enough arranged, the work that gets done isn't very high in either quantity or quality. Coerced workers who cannot rebel or run away nevertheless tend to escape to a certain degree inside themselves. They become apathetic, going dully through the motions that are expected of them but giving nothing beyond the barest minimum. A job that requires any judgment, any initiative, becomes impossible to carry out with coerced labor. You cannot force someone to become a skilled watchmaker by standing over them with a whip, because they will just botch the job. Even with fairly simple work, like smashing rocks on the rock pile, workers who are sufficiently apathetic can work very slowly and sloppily. Even a simple matter like wielding a shovel can be done clumsily.

You might ask why the guards could not just simply beat people into compliance, punishing them if they don't work harder and better. No doubt this is exactly what a slave-labor camp guard would try. But the tactic is somewhat self-defeating. The more one beats the prisoners, the more beaten up they become, the less capable of working harder. Paradoxically, force tends to limit itself. The prisoner who is beaten often is not only physically weaker but also mentally duller. If your management strategy is beating people to a pulp, you will have a pulp working for you. If you beat a worker to death, you don't have any worker at all.

Oddly enough, then, violence works best as an incentive the less it is actually used. Not only does violence tend to make people less capable of doing any work, but it also takes time away from working. If you have to spend all your time beating your workers, you are not getting any work done. Punishment-centered regimes have to hope that the mere threat of violence will terrorize people into working hard. Once they have to start applying the sanctions regularly, their production is going to go rapidly down hill.

An aspect of this comes up in our own lives, far away as we hope we may be from the peasant overseers and slave-drivers of traditional societies, or the concentration camps of the Second World War. Parents have a choice of the same sanctions in controlling their small children. The equivalent of money rewards is giving them candy, or toys, or something else they like. The equivalent of coercion is spanking them. The effects of both are about the same within the family as they are in the factories and prisons we have been discussing just now. If you try to control your kids with candy, you soon find that they become fixated on candy: they won't do anything unless there is a reward attached to it. Similarly, if you try to control them by spanking them, you soon find that this works only to a limited extent. A child who only gets spanked once is much more impressed with it than the child who gets spanked half a dozen times a day. In fact, after a while the punishment becomes almost totally ineffective. In any case, coercion works better in making people *not* do something than motivating positive accomplishments. You can't spank your children into getting good grades at school, and you can't get them to do very much else that way either. What you end up getting instead is a continuously resentful child, who doesn't seem to understand what you are saying to him or her.

The final irony about coercion, in fact, is just this point. Coercing people makes them appear to be stupid. The pattern isn't found only with children; it has been seen over and over again in many different contexts. People who are on the bottom rung of a coercive social system have always had the reputation for being mindless. Russian aristocrats firmly believed that the serfs over whose backs they cracked their whips were stupid people, with no more intelligence than animals. American slave owners of the nineteenth century thought the same about their black slaves. But the same thing was seen in the Nazi and Russian concentration camps. People who went into them might be perfectly ordinary, maybe even brighter than ordinary; after they had been subjected to constant brutality, they began to act dumb as well.

The stupidity is the result of the coercive situation. If there is no possibility of rebellion or escape, prisoners eventually start losing any sense of initiative. Forced to do meaningless work for someone else, they comply in as perfunctory a way as possible. They withdraw as much as they can within a shell. From the outside it looks like stupidity. But it is stupidity only from the viewpoint of the slave-driver, who wishes they would show more initiative on his or her behalf. And that, ultimately, is the slave-driver's stupidity, not theirs.

What all this comes down to is the fact that both rewards and coercion are relatively weak forms of control. If you want to get something done reasonably well, you have to find a way to make people want to do it. That is not to say that rewards and punishments don't play some role in the social world. Obviously pay is very important for at least getting people to take a job, and the threat of punishment has an effect in keeping them from automatically walking off with the contents of the cash register. But if you want to go beyond this minimum, you need some way to get people involved in identifying with the organization and the job. You need to make them feel that the work is part of their own identity, that they are contributing to something they believe in or some group that they belong to.

This is not impossible. In fact, we've already seen one way in which this comes about. It is through social rituals, which create a sense of group identity and produce ideals that people respect. But how do you get social rituals to operate in the world of work?

One way it can be done is to use an organization that is already highly ritualized. The church, for example, controls its own members because they are indoctrinated with the church's purposes by their constant participation in its ceremonies. Priests carry out their duties because they are above all ritual duties, and the rituals affect their own beliefs as well as the beliefs of others. This kind of organizational solidarity can sometimes be put to work for other purposes. The monks can spend their spare time making liqueurs in the wine-cellar, let us say. And in fact, in the Middle Ages, Christian monasteries (and in Asia, Buddhist monasteries, too) did much useful work in both farming and manufacturing.

Highly traditionalized organizations like the church are no longer so important in the economy, but it is possible for organizations to create their own rituals. An army officer corps, for instance, derives a good deal of its motivation from the rituals they go through as military cadets and in the honors of military protocol. An organization like the Marine Corps makes a great deal of its heroic image and constantly puts on various ritual tests of its *machismo* to remind its members of what Marines are supposed to be like. The high-status professions of today make heavy use of rituals in socializing their new members. Medical students, for instance, do not actually learn very much practical medicine in medical school, but they do undergo a lengthy rite of passage that separates them in their own minds from ordinary human beings and makes them take on the special status claims and demeanor of being a doctor. Because of this self-indoctrination, the physician ends up with a very strong identification with the job, and external forms of control over medical practitioners are virtually nonexistent.

At a somewhat less privileged occupational level, rituals are equally important in creating enough solidarity with the organization to keep it functioning. Office workers, as we've seen, are not really very closely controlled by the payment system, but they nevertheless tend to do their work at least up to a certain level of competency. This is largely because they participate in a series of small but significant social rituals that make them identify with their jobs and with the other people in the organization. As Goffman has shown us, there are innumerable small rituals in everyday life in which people act out a particular image of themselves and get other people to accept that image.

The most important of these rituals for the purpose of getting people to identify with their jobs are occasions in which they have to take public responsibility for acting on the part of the organization. This happens whenever someone has to take the role of explaining the organization's policy to an outsider or when someone gives orders to a subordinate. In both these ways, by the taking responsibility for stating the organization's position to other people, that person feels like a part of the organization.

A major way to get people to want to do their job, then, is to give them some responsibility. Above all, this must be a responsibility that is social: put them in a position where they will have to deal with someone else in the name of the organization. This creates loyalty, and makes monetary and coercive controls much less important.

If this method works so well, why isn't it used more often? Why isn't everyone socialized by this soft form of ritual control so that everyone does what they should be doing? The fact is that there are drawbacks. For one thing, rituals take a certain amount of time and effort, and they themselves are not necessarily directly productive. The more time spent on rituals, the less time there is left to actually get work done. The other drawback is that because the most effective rituals are those in which someone has a share in the organization's power, then the more rituals you use, the more power you give away. If everyone in an organization was given some responsibility for giving orders or announcing policies publicly, there would be very little power left for the manager to exercise.

So there is an unavoidable limit in the use of rituals as a form of control. Beyond a certain point, they distract from actually getting work done, and they weaken rather than enhance central control. For these reasons, most organizations use ritual controls only sparingly, and for some positions more than others. The white-collar levels, and especially their higher ranks, are much more ritualized than the lower levels of manual work. For the latter, most organizations rely most heavily on monetary controls. For all their drawbacks, they are on the balance cheaper than trying to ritualize the whole organization.

THE IMPORTANCE
OF THE TAKEN-FOR-GRANTED

The truth seems to be that none of the three forms of control works without very serious limitations. This is not to say that there is no such thing as power. But power is a matter of degree, never an absolute. Some people manage to acquire more power than others, but they have to work for it in many rather subtle ways. The most effective kinds of control are those that operate indirectly. The direct, brutal control via sheer force is the most obvious kind of power, but also the least effective for getting things done. Monetary power, too, is more apparent than real. Ritual power works better precisely because it is covert, though by its very nature it is relatively hard to manipulate. Using rituals usually means actually giving away direct power in return for a more generalized compliance.

The main way in which an organizational politician can exercise power over what other people do is by influencing what they take for granted. This is possible above all for the kinds of reasons that we have already examined in explaining the limits of human rationality. The basic point is that any conscious decision that anyone makes rests upon some unconscious premises. The part that is taken for granted, moreover, is necessarily and

permanently beneath the surface. Human cognition just happens
to be limited in that way. A clever power-seeker plays upon that
limitation.

Try this experiment some time. When you are talking to
someone, make them explain everything they say that isn't completely clear. The result, you will discover, is a series of unin-
terrupted interruptions:

A: Hi, how are you doing?
B: What do you mean when you say "how"?
A: You know. What's happening with you?
B: What do you mean, "happening"?
A: Happening, you know, what's going on.
B: I'm sorry. Could you explain what you mean by "what"?
A: What do you mean, what do I mean? Do you want to talk
to me or not?

It is obvious that this sort of questioning could go on end-
lessly, at any rate if the listener doesn't get very angry and
punch you in the mouth. But it illustrates two important points.
First, virtually everything can be called into question. We are
able to get along with other people not because everything is
clearly spelled out, but because we are willing to take most
things people say without explanation. Harold Garfinkel, who
actually performed this sort of experiment, points out that there
is an infinite regress of assumptions that go into any act of social communication. Moreover, some expressions are simply not
explainable in words at all. A word like "you," or "here," or
"now" is what Garfinkel calls "indexical." You have to know
what it means already; it can't be explained.

"What do you mean by 'you'?"

"I mean *you, you!*" About all that can be done here is point
your finger.

The second point is that people get mad when they are
pressed to explain things that they ordinarily take for granted.
This is because they very quickly see that explanations could

go on forever and the questions will never be answered. If you really demanded a full explanation of everything you hear, you could stop a conversation from ever getting past its first sentence. The real significance of this for a sociological understanding of the way the world is put together is not the anger, however. It is the fact that people try to avoid these sorts of situations. They tacitly recognize that we have to avoid these endless lines of questioning. Sometimes small children will start asking an endless series of "whys," but adults discourage this.

In sum, any social arrangement works because people avoid questioning it most of the time. That does not mean that people do not get into arguments or dispute about just what ought to be done from time to time. But to have a dispute already implies there is a considerable area of agreement. An office manager may dispute with a clerk over just how to take care of some business letter, but they at any rate know more or less what they are disputing about. They do not get off into a Garfinkelesque series of questions over just what is meant by everything that is said. You could very quickly dissolve the organization into nothingness if you followed that route: there would be no communication at all, even about what the disagreement is over.

Social organization is possible because people maintain a certain level of focus. If they focus on one thing, even if only to disagree about it, they are taking many other things for granted, thereby reinforcing their social reality. Thus, even though the boss is arguing with the clerk over just what the instructions are that are supposed to be carried out regarding business letters, the argument simultaneously implies that the boss has the right to give orders and the clerk ordinarily obeys them. Even if the boss loses this particular argument, he or she wins a tacit victory that helps uphold his or her authority in general.

It is in this tacit dimension that power is most effectively carried out, e.g., clever politicians manage to win points in the very process of giving in on something less important.

Power sometimes operates as well by the simple tactic of disrupting any challenge to it. Political debaters know this well enough. If you want to derail your opponents' argument, you interrupt them before they have gotten to their main point and ask them to define their terms. This can easily lead to a side debate that keeps the main argument from ever being reached. Every dispute about what something means has the potential for an infinite regress of questioning. A related tactic is to raise questions on a different level than what your opponents wish to talk about. They want to talk about their proposal or air their grievance; you question the speaker's qualifications, whether other people ought to be represented in order to have a full say in the matter, whether their motivation is sincere in bringing this up, and so forth.

Talk, to use Goffman's analogy again, is like a series of picture frames. You can talk about what is inside the picture, or you can talk about the frame. The picture is the original topic, whatever someone wanted to talk about; the frame is the fact that somebody in particular is talking about it. If you shift the frame into the focus of your conversation, you have put a frame around the frame. Goffman has pointed out many ways in which one can keep on doing this, putting virtually infinite frames around frames around frames. Part of the exercise of power is just this matter of controlling what frame you allow other people to operate within.

These tacit aspects of power all play upon the fundamental limitation of human cognitive capacity: it is not possible to think of all levels at once. Focusing on one thing necessarily pushes others things into the realm of the taken-for-granted. A clever boss or politician tries to take advantage of this situation, to try to make sure that the things he or she is most concerned about become part of the realm that others take for granted.

But there is a limit to this strategy, too. Those in control, as well as those being controlled—workers or constituents—are subject to these same cognitive limitations. The boss has to play it by ear; there is no absolutely optimal way to exercise even these indirect controls. To a certain extent, everyone is caught in the same bind.

OPTIMIZING VERSUS SATISFICING

Take the issue of how to run a factory or a store, or how to keep the paperwork flowing smoothly through an office. Suppose you are the manager. You would like everything to work as well as possible. Your aim is to achieve the optimum level of efficiency.

The question then arises: what is this optimum level? You cannot simply say, turn out as much work as possible. There are other considerations. Shouldn't the work be of high quality? Already there is something of a dilemma. As mentioned before, the faster you have people work, the lower the quality of what they do. Yet, you have to reach some point beyond which you are not willing to sacrifice speed for quality. Where do you set that point?

And this isn't the only trade-off that you will have to calculate. There is, of course, the question of cost. Everyone would like to keep costs down and avoid waste. But just how important are costs compared to everything else? Are you willing to incur a little extra cost in order to make things move as fast as possible? On the other hand, you have a commitment to a certain level of quality. How much are you going to let the costs rise to keep up quality? How much quality is it worthwhile sacrificing in order to keep costs down?

As if this weren't enough, there is more to worry about. What about the safety of your workers? Do you try to maximize that, no matter how slow it forces you to set production or how expensive it is? What about the effects of your operation on the external environment (e.g., if you run a factory that produces fumes or has to dispose of industrial wastes)? How much weight do you give to this, compared to all the other factors we have considered?

Besides these purely technical considerations, you have to bear in mind that the people who will carry out your plans are human. You may set a particular work level, calculating speed, costs, supplies, quality, and all the rest, but the question remains whether you can actually get your workers to carry it out. If you press them too hard, they may strike or quit or just plain fail to perform. You have to worry about all the various incentive systems I have discussed and take each as yet another source of possible cost as well as a draw upon your time and effort. Control by money wages is an obvious cost, and it would be efficient to keep this down as much as possible. But it is not so easy to do this, and monetary controls are not really so very effective in creating compliance anyway. On the other hand, coercion has its obvious drawbacks, and control by rituals is time-consuming and not easy to bring off. The work force, then, is going to be another round of problems to mesh with all the others.

Being a manager, as we have seen, could be a bit of a headache. You have all sorts of things to worry about, and you are supposed to try to be efficient and make the best out of all of them. How do you achieve maximal efficiency? The answer that organizational theory has arrived at is simply this: *there is no such thing as a pure optimal solution to a situation of great complexity.*

What does this mean? It means you are caught in a network of interlocking dilemmas. If you try to optimize one thing, you sacrifice something else. Moreover, many of these processes involve uncertainties that you simply cannot control in advance. How are you going to schedule an organization's work load, for example? You could run a factory to turn out as much as possible right now, but it may happen that next week your raw materials will run short or shipments of fuel won't come in on time. Or it may be that the market will dry up, and you can't sell what you have. Wouldn't it be better to slow down, pace yourself, and try to keep the inflows and outflows balanced fairly smoothly?

Certainly it would be nice to do this, if only you knew just exactly what future supplies and demands were going to be. If you guess wrong about the future, either in the direction of underestimating or overestimating, you will incur some inefficiencies. In any situation where there are many contingencies to deal with, these sorts of problems will arise. If you have many parts to assemble, many products to sell, many different workers to coordinate, there will be continual choices of how to fit things together. And there will be no straight-forward plan that will take care of all contingencies. When various things are all tied together, any unexpected foul-up in one area will hold things up all along the chain.

Now this does not mean that it is impossible to run an organization. Obviously, people do it every day, with a fair degree of success. The point, though, is that it can't be done by setting up a plan that is designed to maximize all aspects of productivity and then following it out to the letter. In fact, the only way you can run a complex organization is to give up on the optimizing strategy. In the words of the Nobel Prize winner Herbert Simon, you do not *maximize* but *satisfice*.

What does this mean? Instead of trying to get the maximum level of productivity, the lowest possible cost, the highest possible quality, the best possible safety record, and so forth, you establish a different criterion. You set a *satisfactory* level for each object, below which you are not willing to accept the outcomes. As long as things meet that satisfactory level, you let things be. In other words, you don't try to have the largest possible output, but instead you set a certain target that you try to meet. You do the same for quality levels, costs, labor relations, safety, and all the rest. How do you know what a satisfactory level should be? Basically, you learn it by trial and error, as whatever emerges from experience.

Once you have these satisfactory levels set, you are now free to spend your attention on whatever seems most important. Part of this involves *troubleshooting*. You have to keep checking to make sure the satisfactory levels are being met in all areas. When one thing falls below that level, that is where you must get to work to correct it. The manager is like a middle linebacker, plugging up the holes in the defensive line wherever they emerge.

This strategy of *satisficing* and *troubleshooting* is the most rational way of dealing with a situation of complexity and uncertainty. To strive for a purely fictional level of absolute efficiency, under these circumstances, would not be more rational, but less. The complexity of an organization is simply greater than the human capacity to process information. Human cognitive limitations do not allow the social world to work like a machine. Instead, we must adapt to our limitations by following a more defensive strategy, which lets many things be partially out of control in return for allowing us to keep things for the most part within acceptable bounds.

Since we live in an era of highly advanced technology, though, we might think of an obvious objection. Perhaps this problem exists for purely human managers, one might say. But why couldn't a computer solve it? Computers have much greater information-processing capacities than humans and should be able to calculate complex interrelationships, even when we can't.

This is an interesting objection because it makes us examine the nature of rationality in general, and not just in human beings. The answer is that computers do not really change anything fundamental in the problem of making decisions in situations of great complexity. What computers are good at is precisely the very routine and predictable operations. They are a big help with speeding up airline reservations, for example, or printing out bank statements, precisely because these are relatively routine and uncomplex operations. There may be large amounts of information to be assembled and coordinated from many different places, and electronic machinery can save a great deal of human effort on these sorts of tasks. But in the realm of complex planning of interacting processes with many unpredictable factors, computers can do no better than humans.

The problem is not that a computer cannot handle large amounts of information. It is just the opposite. The computer is able not only to take in a large quantity of information but also to put out a very large quantity. Where we want a simple an-

swer, the computer will nevertheless give us a very complex
one. Consider a computer programmed to play chess. Presumably a computer should be much better at this than a human
being. After all, it can calculate much faster just what may happen if you take a knight with your queen's bishop's pawn, etc.
and then your opponent could move his or her rook, etc.

But that is exactly the difficulty. You can easily program a
computer to figure out all the possible moves that will follow
after each of your possible moves. Supposing you have 12 possible moves, and your opponent has 12 possible things to do in
response to each move. That makes 144 possible combinations
just for the next exchange of moves. If you follow this out even
3 moves into the future, you get 12^6 possible combinations
(2,985,984), and that is only scratching the surface. An average
game of chess takes some 40 to 60 moves. If you want a computer to calculate a whole game, it would take an incredibly
long time, much longer than you would be alive.

So when you program a chess-playing computer, you build in
one of the limitations that human beings already have. It simply
isn't useful for us to make a computer use its full calculating
capacities, so we only allow it to calculate the consequences of
any move, say, half a dozen exchanges into the future. To let it
run on any further than that would be to provide ourselves with
more information than we can handle.

This kind of limitation actually makes the computer a better
chess player. Even so, computers are not really very good at
playing chess. High-level human chess masters usually have no
difficulty in beating a computer. Why? Because a computer,
operating by brute force of its calculating capacities, is actually
wasting most of its time; the human follows a more definite
strategy, recognizing overall patterns, and building an arrangement on the board that eventually constricts what an opponent
can do. So to program a really good chess-playing computer,
the programmer has to know the best chess strategies and must
figure a way to build them into the computer. One of the in-
venters of the computer, Turing, was never able to create a

computer program that could beat a good human chess player. Turing himself thought that this meant computers could never do everything humans could, although other computer engineers decided that all it meant was that Turing himself wasn't a very good chess player.

Chess playing is a fairly good analogy to the problems that a computer faces in trying to project the proper strategy for an organization. The analogy is weak in that in chess all the possible moves are given, and nothing unexpected can come up that isn't already in the system. But even within these limits, we can see why even the power of electronic calculation cannot arrive at a single strategy that will maximize attainment of all organizational aims. The computer will not come to a single solution but will give a range of solutions—different scenarios based on different possible inputs and different tradeoffs among an organization's different goals. The human managers still have to make their choices among the different scenarios. And even these can go awry, as the experience of big organizations in recent years has shown: automobile companies can still badly miscalculate their markets and lose billions of dollars; the Pentagon still fails in military operations, and wastes all manner of time, materiel, and money during peacetime. Introducing computers into these situations tends to make managerial problems even harder because the computer office is one more segment added onto the organization, making it still more complex to contend with.

So even in a world of computers the final problems of decision-making do not go away. Satisficing remains the best strategy. People may not be able to think like a computer, but it turns out that even a computer can't really think like a computer. The limits on sheer rationality are everywhere.

THE POWER OF UNCERTAINTY

Exactly who emerges from this sort of situation as a holder of power? Everyone has limits on how well they can carry out what they want to accomplish. Any large organization is a maze of contingencies, and its members all stare at invisible walls made up of their own cognitive limitations. Power in these circumstances can be only a matter of degree. Can we say anything about who comes out on top as *relatively* most powerful though?

We can indeed. One of the major generalizations that has emerged from the study of various organizations and professions is that the most powerful positions are those which control some crucial area of uncertainty.

This was first discovered when sociologists were investigating the role of the staff expert in a bureaucracy. The staff expert has no official power; he or she only gives advice to the manager who holds line authority. Nevertheless, it was found that the "staff versus line" distinction was not such a crucial one after all. A staff adviser could often determine what decision the line manager should make by explaining just what the problem is in such a way that only a particular decision could follow.

For example, an engineer or an economist could present their data so that it would appear that only a particular course of action was reasonable. Not all experts always had this power, however. What made the difference was how *routine* the problem appeared to be. If it was a type of problem that came up over and over again, the manager could usually make the judgment alone, and the technical advice of the expert was less influential. But if the problem was in an area of great uncertainty, the expert who defined just what the problem consisted of became very powerful. Paradoxically, this meant that the better the expertise, the less likely the expert was to be powerful. That is because the absolutely fool-proof expert could easily solve the problem whenever it came up, thereby eliminating the uncertainty and turning the area into a routine. Experts in areas in which their expertise still could not reduce the problem to manageable proportions, on the other hand, are the ones whose advice has the most effect on what other people will do.

Thus a lawyer advising a corporation on routine matters would have relatively little influence on policy in general. But the same lawyer could be a very powerful figure if he or she were involved in a delicate negotiation in a case in which it was completely uncertain what the judge might do or what the opposing lawyer would come up with. This kind of case puts the manager of the company in a situation of anxiety and uncertainty, and hence he or she is much more likely to lean heavily on the expert's opinion. And since the whole issue is fuzzy and its boundaries unclear, the lawyer has a good deal of leeway for introducing personal interpretations and influencing the company policy in a range of ways.

This pattern generally holds true. It is those with a unique access to an area of uncertainty affecting other people who have the greatest influence over them. These same experts may not really be able to deal with the uncertainty, but they are able to put other people at their mercy in interpreting what is going on. This dependence shades over into more general feelings of respect toward them and can be translated into covert power.

This is the reason why some professions are so much more powerful than others. When you get right down to it, auto mechanics are a good deal more reliable than doctors at being able to repair what is wrong in their respective spheres. But for that very reason, the skills of a mechanic are not held in very high regard. It is too easy for you to expect that the car should be fixed by tomorrow morning, and if it isn't you go to another mechanic. But doctors deal with illnesses that are much harder to diagnose and treat; if a doctor fails to cure you—especially by any particular deadline—most people will assume it is the fault of the disease and not of the doctor. Medicine is more mysterious than auto mechanics, and that is a major reason for the greater prestige and power of the physician.

Part of the art of holding power is making what you do seem as mysterious and impressive as possible. Doctors maintain a sharp barrier between their own backstage activities and the public they serve; the mysteriousness of medical knowledge is partly a result of the specialized terminology used and the unwillingness of physicians to take the public into their confidence.

Secrecy is even more crucial for politicians in maintaining their power and prestige. A high government official gains tremendously by being able to tell the public he or she is dealing with an international crisis, the details of which cannot be announced for security reasons. Politicians try to wrap what they do in an air of importance. Maintaining secrecy is a way of increasing the drama of what they do, as well as of making it more inaccessible to outsiders. On top of this, politicians genuinely do deal with matters that are uncertain: the way foreign governments are going to react, the way an economic negotiation will turn out, the possible alliances that can be made with other politicians on a vote. Politicians, above all, are dealers in uncertainties, and that is the essence of their power.

We ought to note, finally, that the power of uncertainty can be found at lower levels of an organization as well as at its top level of officials and advisers. In some factories, for example, the maintenance and repair workers have a great deal of power. While everyone else does their job according to a strict routine, they are called into action only when something breaks down. When that happens, they are the only ones who know what needs to be done to put the factory back into operation. They can do it quickly or slowly, and can bargain with the managers for their cooperation, because they alone can really judge just how serious the problem is. Through a subtle bargaining process, they can trade off this power for influence over other aspects of the organization's life.

Many other jobs within organizations at the middle and even lower levels have some aspects of this sort of power. The secretary who opens the boss's mail can have tremendous influence over which matters come to his or her attention and which ones wait their turn. All this is covert power, depending upon being able to define a situation to the people in authority. Since the boss can't see first hand what sort of information is coming in, people who sit astride the communications channels have much hidden influence.

Power within an organization, then, is subject to all sorts of contingencies. It may be that quite a few people control their own areas of information, and many different areas of uncertainty may pop up. Whenever complex things are being carried on and the organization is trying to meet several goals at once, as we have seen, the manager is unable to arrive at any one optimum policy and must consent to satisficing. Satisficing is a strategy forced upon people because of the limitations of multiple uncertainties. The boss is limited to having his or her way in a few areas and leaving other things up to the "normal" levels of operations. These "normal," "satisfactory" levels are in reality established by the exercise of covert power by other people in the organization.

In the final analysis, power turns out to be at least partially an illusion. Some people can give orders, but the orders can only be carried out successfully if they are confined within certain possibilities. And since the boss has to depend on others for information about what is going on, his or her orders always reflect the covert influence of those who supplied the information, and hence defined the situation, in the first place.

Whether this is a happy or sad state of affairs depends on your point of view. From the manager's viewpoint, it is the reason why organizations never seem to run all that smoothly. For anyone who makes policy or wishes that something could be done in a certain way, it is a counsel of pessimistic realism. For people who work in an organization, however, and who are subjected to other people's exercise of power, the looseness of power is a blessing. The paradoxes of power are a principal source of individual freedom.

4

THE NORMALCY
OF CRIME

There have been several widely accepted views about crime. The more obvious explanations begin at the level of common sense. The trouble with common sense, though, is that there are usually opposite opinions on any subject, both of which are equally commonsensical to those who believe in them. These views have generally corresponded to popular political beliefs. Roughly speaking, we may refer to them as the conservative and liberal views on crime. As in other areas of sociology, these obvious explanations do not go very far. Sociological theorists have both criticized these positions and used them in attempts to make them more sophisticated. The main result of this research has been to make us aware of how difficult it is to understand crime, and especially to control it, by following commonsense assumptions. Crime is still here; public outcries about it are as loud as ever.

Other sociological theories have pursued the matter further. But as they have gotten deeper and deeper into the question, the causes of crime have gone from the obvious to the nonobvious. A more radical political stance has generated its own version of a nonobvious understanding of crime, but also raises new problems.

The most sophisticated and least obvious theory of crime, I will suggest, goes back once again to Durkheim. The problem has not turned out to be just what we once thought it was. We may have to face a paradox: crime exists because it is built into the structure of society itself. This does not mean that nothing can be done about it, but the social costs of controlling crime may involve more difficult change than we have been aware of.

CONSERVATIVE EXPLANATIONS OF CRIME

One view of crime is that criminals are simply bad people; the only way to deal with them is to punish them. The more crime there is, the harder we should crack down on it. This position has been held for many centuries, and it keeps on being restated today. The trouble is that it has never really worked. In Europe during the 1600s and 1700s, punishments were as severe as one could imagine. People were hung for stealing a loaf of bread; others were branded or had their ears cut off. Some offenders, especially people accused of religious or political crimes, were tortured to death. All these punishments were public spectacles. A crowd would gather around to watch a good execution, while vendors sold refreshments and people made bets on how long the criminal would yell while he or she was burning at the stake. People today who advocate severe punishments as a deterrent for crime would have been delighted by the situation.

But the brutal punishments did not work. Crime kept right on occurring at a tremendous rate for hundreds of years, despite the hangings and the mutilations. How could this be possible when people were risking such punishments? Very likely it happened because the punishments themselves made people callous. The public executions created a barrier to sympathy between the crowd and the victim on the scaffold. It was some other breed of creature who was dying up there, while the audience enjoyed itself down below. All this official violence must have made people feel that human suffering counted for very little. They became callous even about themselves, so that the violent punishments did not seem like so much of a threat to them as they would to us today. Eventually the extreme punishments were no longer enforced, and finally they were given up entirely.

The same kind of situation still can be found in some parts of the world today. In Saudi Arabia and some other Muslim countries, theft is punished by cutting off a hand, and many other offenses by death. Executions are carried out in public, with the whole community required to attend. But the results are the same as they were in medieval Europe. These rural Muslim communities have very high murder rates. Much of this is probably due to the callous attitude toward human life that is produced by their system of legal punishment. A good deal of the violence of these societies, moreover, does not even show up in the murder statistics for it is sanctioned by common custom. Many of the victims are women, killed by their husbands, brothers, or fathers for the crime of "adultery": under strict traditional morality, this can be any offense even as mild as talking to a man outside the family. The violent punishments for crime in these societies go along with an authoritarian social structure with strong local ties and ritual barriers between groups. These are patrimonial societies organized around the power of family heads; from a sociological viewpoint, their use of ritualized public violence reflects this social structure.

We can begin to see, therefore, that the philosophy of punishing criminals as violently as possible is not really a policy that people advocate because it has proven effective. It is a political position, or what comes to the same thing, a moral philosophy, which declares it is good to be tough and even brutal or malicious to offenders. Just why people hold this position is itself a question for sociology to explain, since they must hold it for some other reason than its practical effects. The holders of this position doubtless consider it rational, but here again we see that their rationality has a nonrational foundation. They do not bother to look at the evidence for whether severe deterrents work but already "know" their policy is right. This sense of rightness is the mark of a partisan position, in this case political conservatism.

A somewhat more scientific version of this political position has tried to tie crime to biology. Today some assert that criminals have bad genes; their propensities to crime are inborn and, hence, nothing can be done about them. Society could only pick them out at an early age by appropriate testing and then presumably get rid of them in some way. Just how this is to be done is not yet worked out: whether the police would hold a complete dossier on all people with bad genes, or whether such people would be locked up for life, or be sterilized, or even exterminated. The issue hasn't really gotten to this point because the position so far is completely theoretical. No one knows how to make a test for bad genes, and there is no real comparative evidence that such genes are causes of crime. The modern genetic theory of crime is another version of conservative political ideology. This is easy to see, since the same arguments about criminals are also applied to welfare recipients and other social types who are anathema in conservative thinking.

The biological theory of crime is not a new one. A century ago it was popular to say that criminals, as well as beggars and other social failures, were biological defectives. The scientific evidence at that time consisted of taking measurements of the size of people's skulls, which was supposed to be an indication of intelligence. Cranial measurements were dropped after a while, partly because it turned out that smart or dumb people come with all sizes of heads, partly because it was apparent that different head shapes had more to do with different ethnic groups than with crime per se. Eventually, the revulsion against the Nazis, who were very big on putting biological theories into practice, caused most people to shy away from this type of explanation. The fact that biological theories have started coming back today is probably more an indication of how the political tides are turning rather than of any advance in sociological research.

LIBERAL EXPLANATIONS

If there is a conservative version of common sense about crime, there is a liberal common sense as well. The liberal position makes an effort to understand what it is like being in the criminal's shoes. Why would someone enter a life of crime, and what can be done to help them out of it? There have been several answers to these questions.

One is that criminals are people who have gotten in with the wrong crowd. Youths hangs around with a delinquent gang and start to pick up delinquent values themselves. Soon they are committing petty thefts, small acts of vandalism, and the like. This moves them more and more into the delinquent culture, and eventually they move on to serious crimes and become full-fledged criminals.

A similar type of explanation is that criminals come from broken homes and run-down neighborhoods. These childhood stresses and strains make people hostile and insecure, and lead them to a life of crime. Growing up in an area of poverty and disillusionment, these youths have no reason to be attached to normal society. They feel that society has no use for them, and they have every reason to take revenge in any way they can.

Sometimes this argument is taken one step further to propose that it isn't just their background that makes some people become criminals, but also the lack of opportunities to change their social condition. If children from poor families or racial minorities had a chance to rise in the world, they would become normal, productive members of society. It is because they are trapped by the lack of opportunities to get ahead that they turn to crime. It is proposed, moreover, that the social atmosphere of the United States makes this feeling particularly strong. For the U.S. is an achievement-oriented culture, where people are expected to make a success on their own. Presumably because of this pressure to succeed, those who do not end up feeling especially alienated and take out their resentments in the form of crime.

It has been argued, for example, that the reason why Italian-Americans have been so prominent in organized crime was because they immigrated to America at a time when ethnic discrimination was strong. Previously arriving ethnic groups, like the Irish in the big cities, held most of the lower-level municipal jobs, including the positions on the police force. With all the expectations of economic success in America, but facing a lack of legitimate opportunities, many Italians turned to an illegitimate route to make their fortunes. The Mafia, thus, is a round-about way of trying to live up to the American dream.

A version of this line of thought even suggests that the schools are indirectly responsible for a good deal of juvenile delinquency. The schools are the place where the official getting-ahead-by-your-own-merits ideal is most strongly pushed. Because of the widespread demand for upward mobility opportunities, we have reached the point in recent decades at which virtually all children are encouraged to stay in school through high school graduation, if not beyond. Nevertheless, it is clear to most students that not everyone is going to go equally far in the system. Some have the academic aptitude, the motivation, the social skills, and the contacts to get ahead, while others do not. Some students are in high school because they are on the beginning steps of a career, while others are just going through the motions while waiting to get out. The experience of being forced to be in school but getting nothing out of it, according to this interpretation, is exactly what creates resentment and juvenile delinquency. It is no wonder, then, that juvenile delinquents often get their start by acts of vandalism like throwing stones through school windows.

Some of these arguments, we can see, get to be rather complicated. Nevertheless, they all share the notion that crime is not really the fault of the criminal. He (or she—although in fact the great majority of criminals are male) would rather not be a criminal if he could help it. It is only the adverse social conditions that force them into a criminal career.

This type of explanation certainly has the appeal of sounding altruistic, and it has given rise to a great many efforts at reform and rehabilitation to set criminals back on the path to normal social participation. This philosophy has dominated official thinking about penal institutions for some time now. Prisons are not supposed to be places for punishment primarily, but places for reform and rehabilitation. Thus a series of reforms has attempted to clean up the prisons, eliminate brutal punishments on the part of the guards, and provide recreational and educational facilities. Prisons supposedly have become places where criminals can learn a useful trade, acquire a high school degree, or otherwise fit themselves for a normal career once they get back outside. In connection with this, parole boards have expanded their functions. It is felt that it is better for convicted criminals to be out of prison and back in the community, under the supervision of a sympathetic parole officer, who guides their readjustment to a useful and productive life.

In this way, all of the various social causes that are believed to account for crime are to be counteracted by an appropriate social reform. If it is a delinquent milieu that starts youth on their evil ways, we provide youth services and group workers to try to lure the gangs off the streets and onto supervised playgrounds. For broken homes and run-down neighborhoods, there are social workers and urban renewal projects. For blocked mobility opportunities, there are various efforts to improve the life chances of the disadvantaged, to keep them in school longer, to provide remedial services, and the like.

As I said, all of this is very altruistic, but it has one big drawback. It simply has not worked very well. Liberal social programs have been in effect for a number of decades now, but the crime rate has not fallen. On the contrary, the index of most crimes proportionate to the population has gone up in the last twenty years. None of the social programs for preventing crime has apparently had much effect.

One can see this by looking at the programs one by one as well as overall. Youth group workers, say, or parole officers have not had much success in countering criminal cultures. Youth workers may be able sometimes to befriend a gang, but they do not really change its ways; and parole officers are just one more fixture in the life of ex-convicts, along with their other kinds of criminal connections. The rehabilitation-oriented prison clearly is a failure. In fact, there is considerable evidence that prisons are likely to confirm many prisoners in a criminal career, precisely because they become involved in a social group of other prisoners who uphold a criminal style of life. Prisons are dominated by tough gangs of prisoners, usually organized on racial and ethnic lines—the Black Muslims, the Mexican Mafia, the Aryan Brotherhood—that settle their own feuds privately and violently, organize homosexual rapes, and provide drugs and other illegal services in the prisons. These same organizations continue to operate once convicts leave prison. For many of them there these may be the strongest social connections they have. Ironically, the prison not only does not rehabilitate criminals, but it often provides an organizational base which allows ex-prisoners to most easily continue their criminal careers. Hence, it is not too surprising to discover that about 40 percent of ex-prisoners return to prison within a few years after their release.

These sorts of facts are a fairly serious indictment of the liberal theories of crime and its prevention, but this hasn't entirely convinced the proponents of these theories that they are wrong. They can continue to argue, for example, that the proper counteractive measures have not been applied vigorously enough. We need more youth group workers, they may reply, or a more extensive attack on the existence of poverty and racial discrimination, or a more serious effort to create career mobility opportunities for deprived youth and ex-convicts alike. This has some plausibility since it is certainly true that much more could be done in this altruistic direction. But the suspicion has been growing that the underlying theories just may not be accurate. Take the broken-family-and-blighted-neighborhood hypothesis about crime. This explanation seems to fit our commonsense view of the world: stress and deprivation lead to crime. But the evidence does not exactly bear this out. Not everyone from a divorced family becomes a criminal; in fact, most such children do not. This is especially apparent today, when divorce has become a normal and accepted part of otherwise quite average families. Nor is it fair to say that everyone who lives in a poor neighborhood is a criminal: again, it is only a minority within this area who are. Hence it cannot be poverty per se that causes crime but some other factor. This becomes even clearer when we realize that by no means are all criminals poor or from racial minorities. Delinquent youths are found in middle-class areas as well as poor ones. Rich boys at fraternity parties commit acts of vandalism, too, as well as violence, rape, theft, and all the rest of it, although they are not always charged with these crimes. The same thing is true among adults. It is not just the poorer social classes that commit crimes. So-called white-collar crime is also a major problem, ranging from passing bad checks to embezzling business funds or conspiring to bribe government officials or to evade legal regulations.

The altruistic, liberal theories of crime are just not adequate to deal with these phenomena. What looked at first glance like a realistic sociological explanation of crime turns out on closer examination not to fit the facts very well at all. There is less crime in the deprived areas of society than the theory would predict and more crime elsewhere in society where these conditions do not hold. It is no wonder, one might conclude, that the liberal methods for preventing crime and rehabilitating criminals have not had much success.

RADICAL EXPLANATIONS OF CRIME

In recent sociology there has been an upsurge of theorizing that rejects the more traditional kinds of theories in favor of a radically new look at the crime issue. Here the theories enter the realm of the nonobvious and even the paradoxical.

The basic turn in the argument has been to shift attention away from the criminal side and to look critically instead at the agents of law-enforcement. For example, it is sometimes argued that increases in the crime rate have nothing to do with how many crimes are actually committed. All that has changed, it is suggested, is that more crimes are being reported. Sometimes a newspaper will create a crime wave by running crime stories more prominently on the front pages—perhaps for political purposes, to attack a city administration or make an issue of the crime problem for an up-coming election. The police, too, it is charged, inflate the crime rate by improving their record-keeping capabilities. Unsolved crimes that formerly were left unreported are now included. This makes a good argument for police appeals that they need an increased budget.

It does appear to be true that some alleged shifts in crime rates are produced in this way. Newspapers in particular are not a very reliable source of information on social trends, and official police statistics are also subject to biases due to shifts in reporting methods. Whenever one sees a rapid jump in crime rates over a space of a year, it is often due to a purely administrative change in the statistical accounting system. At the same time, it has to be said that not all of the shifts in crime rates can be attributed to causes of this sort.

But there is a much more radical sense in which it is proposed that crimes are created by the law-enforcement side. This is referred to as the labeling theory. The argument goes like this. All sorts of youths violate the laws. They engage in petty thefts and acts of vandalism. They get into fights, drink illegally, have illicit sex, smoke dope or use drugs, and so on. This is widespread and almost normal behavior at a certain age. What is crucial, though, is that some of these young people get caught. They are apprehended by the authorities for one thing or another. Now even at this point there is a possibility of heading off the negative social consequences. Some of these youths get off with a warning, because their school principal likes them, say, or because their parents intervene, or because the police are sympa-

thetic to them. If so, then they have escaped going down into
a long funnel at the end of which lies a full-fledged criminal
identity.

If a young offender is actually arrested, charged with a
crime, convicted, and all the rest, this has a crucial effect upon
the rest of his or her career. This happens in several ways. One
effect is psychological: those who had previously regarded
themselves as more or less like anyone else, just goofing off perhaps, now are someone special. They are now labeled an offender, a juvenile delinquent, a criminal; they are caught up in
a network of criminal-processing organizations. Every step along
the way reinforces the sense that they have become someone different from the normal. They acquire a criminal identity.

Once this happens it is hard to dislodge. The person has
passed over the borderline to "the other side," and it becomes
next to impossible to get back again. This is why, for all the
emphasis on rehabilitation, youth counseling, parole officers,
and all the rest, offenders tend to repeat their crimes and often
move on to more serious offenses. Starting with getting caught
for vandalism, say, someone may move on to auto theft. Getting
caught for that, in time, and receiving a more serious sentence,
they are even more deeply embroiled in a criminal identity. The
court proceedings act as a ritual that deepens and confirms their
criminal identity. If they go to prison, they are enclosed in a
milieu of other criminals, so that a criminal outlook and life-
style become the only meaningful world to them. Even if they
do not go to prison (or after they are released), they live in a
world oriented toward the parole officer, with the police and the
courts ever present in the back of their minds. All the things that
liberal, reform-oriented, crime-control agencies do actually serve
to remind the offenders continually of their criminal identity,
and this acts to reinforce it.

In this way, a self-perpetuating chain of criminal activities
builds up. The key point in the whole sequence is right at the
beginning, where the labeling process begins. It is the first, dramatic confrontation with the law that makes all the difference,

deciding which way the individuals will go. Either they will get by with a bit of normal goofing off, or they are embarked on a career of crime in which everything that is done to prevent it actually makes it all the more inevitable.

This is a rather psychological way of describing the dynamics of the labeling process. I could fill in the process from a different angle, one that does not stress so much the shift that takes place within the novice "criminal's" mind but within the organization of the law-enforcement world itself. Sociologists who have studied the police point out that the police constitute an organization, with administrative problems just like any other organization. A business organization needs to keep up its sales; a police organization needs to keep apprehending criminals and solving crimes. This is by no means an easy thing to do. Some crimes are relatively easy to solve, such as murder (we will see why a little further on). But these make up only a small percentage of total crimes. The most common crimes, and those which most widely affect the public, are burglary, auto theft, and other types of larceny. These are hard to solve precisely because there are so many of them. There usually is little evidence left at the scene of the crime, and there are rarely any witnesses. Except when a thief is caught in the act, it is very hard to catch him or her. And even if they are apprehended, it is hard to get evidence that will hold up in court. Since most thefts are carried out alone, for instance, it is not usually possible to get one criminal to testify against another, as is done in other sorts of crimes. How, then, do the police try to control this large category of crime?

The best strategy they can follow is to try to get confessions from the criminals that they do apprehend. So whenever someone is arrested with goods from a burglary, say, a great deal of pressure is put on them to confess to other burglaries. There are all sorts of police interrogation methods, and sometimes a brutal use of force can be one of them. The most effective sort of pressure, though, is usually in the form of a bargain. The accused criminals are encouraged to confess to a list of unsolved thefts;

in return for this, they are allowed to plead guilty to some restricted charge, e.g., one or two counts of burglary, or even some
lesser offense. This is a typical plea bargain. The prosecution
and defense attorneys work out an agreement that they will ask
the judge for a particular sentence, while the rest of the charges
are dismissed. Everyone gets something from this deal. The
criminal gets a light sentence—a year in jail or even just probation. The police get to declare a dozen burglaries solved, which
makes their department look efficient in their annual statistical
report. The prosecuting attorneys cut down their court time,
and the judge gets to move the cases through faster, thereby reducing crowding in the overworked courts. The only ones who
do not benefit from the system are the robbery victims, who
don't get their property back and don't receive any real protection in the form of apprehending the real offenders.

All this has a powerful effect in reinforcing the "labeling"
process that keeps people going in criminal careers. The way
police can make their system work is to keep tabs on people
whom it is easiest to arrest. As I said, it is hard to find the particular burglar who was responsible for the latest round of break-
ins. He or she (but usually he) would be especially hard to find
if new to the scene. The easiest people to arrest, on the other
hand, are people who have been arrested before. So one way police can "solve" a round of burglaries is to pay a surprise call on
formerly convicted criminals in the area who are out on parole.
One of the conditions of parole often is that the ex-convict should
be subject to search. So the police arrive, look for stolen property, illegal drugs, or other violations. Often it is not hard to find
these, especially since drugs of one kind or another are generally a part of the criminal culture. (Which is not to say that
these same drugs may not also be part of the life-style of people
who are not in the criminal world.)

So the police then are able to set the bargaining process in
motion. A former criminal, especially one on parole, is particularly vulnerable, since a condition of parole is to avoid any similar criminal violations. Any violation of parole revokes their

freedom and sends them back to prison to finish their sentence. This puts considerable pressure on the parolee to agree to a lengthy confession to clear the police record, in return for a plea-bargain granting some leniency. The result is another round of probation or prison, parole, and so forth.

Thus, the chain of events that starts when someone is labeled a criminal for some initial offense, can end up as a kind of invisible prison in its own right. Once someone becomes known to the police, they are subject to organizational pressures that will send them through the system over and over again. Whether they come to strongly identify themselves personally with a criminal identity or not, the police will tend to do so, and that makes it all the harder to get out. Ex-convicts are trapped in a machine that constantly reprocesses them because they are its easiest materials to reach.

The labeling theory declares that crime is actually created by the process of getting caught. Unlike the previous types of theories that we looked at, the personal characteristics of the individuals, or their social class or ethnic or neighborhood background, is not a crucial point. It is assumed that all sorts of people violate the law. But only some of them get caught, are prosecuted, labeled and all the rest, thereby becoming full-fledged criminals. If criminals who go through the courts and the prisons are so often likely to be disproportionately poor, black, or otherwise fit someone's idea of "social undesirables" or the "socially deprived," it is because these are the types of people who are most likely to be apprehended and prosecuted. The fraternity boys stealing a college monument or raping the sorority girls at a party are let off with a reprimand because these are labelled "college pranks." The poor black youth who does the same sort of thing gets sent to juvenile court and a start on a career of serious crime.

There is an even stronger version of the radical approach to crime. This argues that it is not simply the police who create the criminals but the law itself. To cite an obvious example: possession of drugs such as narcotics was not a crime until laws were passed making private possession of them a felony. In the 1800s, the use of opium and opiate-based preparations such as laudanum was not illegal, and it was fairly widespread. The drugs could be bought over the counter at a pharmacy. Many people used them in patent medicines. Others used them for pain-killers, escape, or because they liked the sensations they produced. The same was true of hashish and marijuana, or of coca and cocaine, which were used in greater or lesser quantities by various kinds of people. In the early 1900s, the public use of opium and its derivatives was outlawed in the United States, and under a series of international agreements, by most of the modern states around the world. Other laws followed, outlawing cocaine and cannabinols.

These laws suddenly created a new category of crime. People who had previously been engaging in a purely private act were now breaking a fairly serious law. This had a great many social ramifications. For one thing, the labeling processes outlined above, both psychological and organizational, were set in motion. People caught for a drug offense could now be siphoned into a criminal milieu and caught up in a criminal career. Whereas formerly opium might be taken by elderly spinsters for their cough, or enjoyed in an average working-class tavern, now the opiate seeker had to inhabit an underground of street scenes, secret meetings with drug dealers, and, of course, the ever-present spectre of the police.

The illegalizing of drugs, moreover, had an important economic effect. When drugs were sold on the open market, their cost was relatively low because they are relatively inexpensive to produce and transport. But when drugs became illegal, the whole business was greatly restricted. As one can see from a simple application of the economics of supply and demand, restricting the supply raised the price. Whereas a modest supply of opium in early nineteenth-century England cost a shilling (the equivalent of perhaps $25 today), heroin (a twentieth-century derivative of opium) now costs some $2000 an ounce. Drug dealers and smugglers incur much greater expenses, keeping their activities hidden as much as possible, paying out bribes, and also paying for the inevitable legal fees when they are caught. So the illegalizing of drugs, by raising the prices, ramified into many other crimes that had formerly been unconnected with the drug market. Smuggling and bribery expanded, of course, but so did burglary and robbery. Most drug addicts, unable to pay for the expense of supporting a costly opiate habit, turned to theft as a main way of keeping the money coming in. From the initial decision to outlaw drugs, then, many other crimes followed.

The same kind of analysis has been applied to many other sorts of crimes. The national prohibition of alcohol in the United States, which held sway between 1919 and 1933, for example, created a whole illegal culture of speak-easies, stills, alcohol smugglers, and an organized crime network to "protect" these operations. These were essentially business activities, bringing in a regular flow of money; but as I noted in an earlier chapter, business contracts cannot be upheld without something to enforce them, and in this case the regular court and police systems were not available since these business activities had become illegal. Instead what appeared were illegal "enforcers" in the persons of Al Capone and other Mafia chieftains. As in so many of these instances, creating one type of crime tended to create other crimes as well.

The outlawing of gambling has had similar effects. Here, sociologists have come up with some interesting materials on how the illegal and the legal worlds interact. Illegal bookmakers are left without the protection of the law, and hence they are prey to criminal gangs who extort money from them for "protection." Whom the gangs guaranteed protection from, however, was usually themselves: if the gamblers didn't pay up, the gang would smash up their office and beat up the bookies. As the gangs grew more sophisticated, they discovered that they did not need to become involved in the violence themselves; it was better to keep things quiet, since violence draws too much public attention. If a bookie refused to pay protection money, then, all the gang had to do was to tip off the police to raid the gambling operation. Contemporary organized crime thus operates in symbiosis with the police, rather than in opposition to it. After all, it is because gambling is illegal that organized criminals can run a protection racket. Far from being in favor of a liberalization of the law, criminals of this sort need the law to make their own livelihood possible. In the same way, not everyone in the illegal drug business is necessarily in favor of decriminalizing drugs. The prices of opiates, cocaine, or marijuana would drop enormously if they could be sold legally. Once again, the huge fortunes that successful smugglers and large-scale dealers can make would no longer be available.

The radical approach to the analysis of crime turns up a great many ironic interconnections between crime and the social structure. Actions taken by citizens in the name of morality and law-abidingness add up to vastly increasing the amount of criminality. Some sociologists have argued that an explanation of crime really boils down to an explanation of how certain things came to be defined as crimes. It has been suggested that crimes are manufactured by "moral entrepreneurs," people who try to create a morality and enforce it upon others. Other sociologists have gone farther, to look for the economic and organizational interests or the social movements that create crimes in this way. It may be suggested, for example, that the outlawing of drugs in the early twentieth century was part of the efforts of the medical profession to monopolize control over all drugs for itself. The prohibitionist movement has been explained as a last-ditch effort of rural Anglo-American Protestants to try to head off what they saw as the degenerate alcoholic culture of the immigrants in the big cities. An analysis along these lines could be applied to current movements that are attempting to create new definitions of crime, such as the antiabortion movement.

At this point, one might step back and ask a question. The examples given have all been of the type of activities that offend some people's moral sense as to what is proper. Drug taking, drinking, gambling—one could add prostitution, pornography, homosexuality and other sexual practices—all involve people who willingly consent to these actions. These actions offend only outsiders. They are what are called "victimless crimes." Here the idea that society creates these crimes in a fairly arbitrary sense, just by passing a law against them, has a good deal of plausibility. But what about "real" crimes, such as robbery, murder, assault, rape, and all other actions that hurt someone's life, body, or property? One could well maintain that these actions would not be considered licit by most people, even if there were no laws prohibiting them. These seem to be "natural," rather than "artificial" categories of crime, and people would want to stop them without the necessity of some kind of moral crusade trying to have laws passed to outlaw them.

However, the most radical position in sociological theory attempts to show that these crimes, too, are socially created. For example, the crime of robbery is only a crime because of the system of property. If there were no private property, it would not be possible to steal it. Moreover, if societies were not stratified on the basis of property into the class that owns the means of production and the class that is forced to sell its labor in order to stay alive, then people would not be motivated to steal. It is the capitalist system that makes some people poor and others rich. Crime, thus, can be seen as one version of the economic class struggle. It is the structure of social class domination that makes property offenses into crimes. By extension, it is argued, other sorts of "serious" crimes—violence, murder, rape—can be explained as part of the situation of a class-stratified society rather than of the natural order of things. If one could eliminate that class domination, one could eliminate crime.

This is certainly a theory worth thinking about. It has the merit of seeing that "real" crimes are a matter of conflict between people in a stratified society, and especially that economic crimes are part of the system of economic stratification in general. Since economic crimes like robbery and auto theft make up the largest proportion of all crimes, this kind of theory can potentially explain a great deal.

Nevertheless, we cannot immediately jump to the conclusion that crime is class struggle of exactly the same sort as usually featured in the Marxian model. For one thing, when we look at who are the victims of crimes, we find a rather surprising pattern. The poorer classes are much more likely to be robbed or burglarized than the wealthier classes. And this is true, in the United States, for both whites and blacks. In fact, blacks with the lowest incomes are the most likely of all to be victims of crimes of virtually all sorts, including murder and rape as well as property crime.

Clearly, then, there is a stratified pattern of crime, but it is not primarily the poor robbing (and murdering and raping) the rich. Criminals are not Robin Hoods. What appears to be going on, rather, is that crime is mainly *local*. People rob, burglarize, murder, and rape in their own neighborhoods above all. The reason is fairly simple: these are the easiest opportunities, especially for teenagers, who commit the majority of all crimes.

The end result is that there is a social-class pattern in crime after all, but it comes out in the fact that neighborhoods tend to be segregated by social class, as well as by race and ethnicity. Hence it is the least privileged people who commit the largest number of crimes, but their victims are primarily people like themselves. It is mainly the poor robbing the poor.

The class-conflict model is relevant, but we actually must push it farther than the Marxists do. For as we saw earlier (in chapter 1), when people are out fighting for their own self-interests, there is no reason why they should trust *anybody*, including people of their own economic class. There is a good deal more conflict than one finds in the Marxian picture of a showdown between two opposing classes. For the working class to fight as a unified class against the bourgeoisie, it would have to have a good deal of solidarity within its own ranks. But that is precisely what is missing in the poorest and most discriminated-against sectors of society. At most, there are small gangs that manage to create solidarity in their own ranks by a great deal of ritualism, such as the fancy handshakes and the verbal games at which black gang members are so adept. But these gangs mainly fight among themselves and prey upon the unorganized people of their own neighborhoods. Insofar as it has no solidarity as a larger group, the lower-class milieu is very much like a war of all against all.

The larger system of economic and racial stratification thus enters into the picture of how crime occurs, but in a roundabout way. Lower-class crime is not primarily class warfare against the higher classes. One can say, though, that the larger stratification of the society has produced the situation in which lower-class crime occurs. The lowest classes, without economic opportunities to make a decent living, and minorities subject to discrimination, have little that ties them into the rest of society. They are the isolated individuals, or at best the isolated small groups, in our society. Without the solidarity that comes from being tied into decent careers, they act mainly as self-interested individuals, without feelings of moral obligation to others. The situation of the lower class, and especially of young, lower-class blacks, illustrates the negative side of the model of solidarity we have examined in earlier chapters of this book. Where social organization fails to create the mechanisms for integrating people into larger group memberships, moral sentiments do not appear. We find instead the situation of mutual distrust and everyone-for-themselves that, as Durkheim argued, would be the result of individuals acting completely on their own self-interest. Recall that in the choice between cheating and obeying the rules, the rational individual, *acting purely as an individual,* would always cheat. That is the situation of a class of people who are deprived of ties to the rest of society.

The class-conflict model makes a certain amount of sense once it is toned down and integrated with the model of how solidarity arises and does not arise. Marxian theory can tell us something if we combine it with Durkheim's. Crime is too individualistic to be straightforward class struggle. But it is the system of class stratification that eliminates the conditions for solidarity in the most depressed sectors of society. Marx, in fact, might well have agreed with this. He was advocating a particular kind of class conflict, one with a great deal of solidarity within the largest social class, and hence he would not have seen crime as any kind of real substitute for class conflict.

The Marxian theory has a practical application. If crime is mainly caused by the economic system, then one would predict that crimes against property would disappear in socialist societies. Since there is no more private property, and everything belongs to the community as a whole, individuals should no longer have any motivation to steal. Evidence on crime in the socialist societies that exist today enables us to test this prediction.

What we find, though, is that theft, murder, rape and other conventional crimes happen in socialist societies at a level that is not greatly different from that in capitalist societies. The police forces have not dwindled away for lack of anything to do. Crime continues to exist in socialist societies. And if we think about it, why after all should it disappear just because property is officially owned by everyone in common? There is still the issue of the individual's interest versus that of the group. As we might have expected from our earlier discussion of the free-rider problem, there is no natural process that automatically makes individuals in a socialist society think that their self-interest coincides with that of the community.

Socialist societies even create new forms of crime, just as the radical theories predict, even though the application may be somewhat unexpected in this case. In a society like the Soviet Union, running a private business for profit is generally a crime (although a few exceptions are made), whereas this would not be so in a capitalist society. Hence socialist societies have a whole category of crime that does not exist elsewhere. It seems that if one creates a criminal category, somehow people will pop up to fill it. Socialist societies have created other new categories of crime as well. Factory managers in the Soviet economy are required to fulfill their production quotas every month, and failure to live up to the demands may result in criminal prosecution as an offense against the state. Since these quotas are continually being raised, most managers are constantly in danger of prosecution. Just as we have seen in the case of the drug laws or gambling laws in our own society, the creation of a category of industrial crime in socialist societies results in all sorts of ancillary crimes being committed as well. Soviet factory managers engage in all sorts of practices to try to make their production levels look satisfactory, including falsifying their records, shifting shipments and deliveries from one month to another, and generally attempting to hold their own against the system. Illegal collusion between officials becomes a normal practice, since superiors cannot help but know what their subordinates are doing, even though they are implicating themselves by not reporting the violations. Bribery emerges in this situation, and out of this other illegal transactions can occur, including shifting some of the public goods to private hands. If we look on both the United States and the USSR from a certain height of abstraction, it appears that there is something about the pressures of the legal system in both that creates a structural equivalent of organized crime.

One could argue, of course, that the Soviet Union is not really a good example of true socialism. It does not come near enough to the ideal of an unstratified society. In the existing soviet-style societies, the state and the communist party seem to have taken the place of the capitalists and provide their own form of domination. Hence, these societies produce their own form of crime, with all its ramifications. The basic point of the radical approach, though, is that crime is caused not by the individuals or their social milieu, but by the enforcement apparatus. It is labeling, or the passing of laws, that creates crimes. From this, it should follow that if one simply abolished crime laws, crime would disappear.

Actually, occasions have arisen when something like this has occurred. Denmark in 1944, for instance, had been conquered by the armies of Nazi Germany. But in that year the Allied British, American, and Canadian forces had landed in France, and the Germans feared a Danish revolt. They arrested all of the

Danish police and left the country without a police force. This situation went on for almost a year, until the Allies finally reached Denmark in 1945. What happened to crime during this period? Certain kinds of crimes rose rapidly. The number of robberies went up to a level ten times as high as usual. For crimes against property, then, it appears that the labeling theory does not necessarily work very well. A society without any law enforcement would not eliminate crime; on the contrary, it would doubtless be a situation in which many people would help themselves to whatever they wanted that other people had. The free-rider problem would be rampant, unless there were some very strong moral feelings throughout the society—a condition that is certainly not very common in most modern societies.

It is interesting to note, though, that the crime rates in Denmark went up only in the category of crimes against property. There was no change in the number of murders or of sex crimes, for instance. These seem to be crimes of passion, motivated in a way that has nothing to do with the enforcement apparatus; other evidence bears this out.

There has been a lot of controversy over the death penalty in recent decades. If we leave aside the moral questions involved in this, and concentrate only on the research that has been done, we can see some interesting patterns. Some states in the U.S. have the death penalty, while others have abolished it. If we compare states that are similar in their social characteristics, it turns out that they have about the same murder rates, whether they have the death penalty or not. That implies that people do not decide to commit murder or not according to whether they expect to risk a severe penalty for it. Murders do not seem to be related to any social calculus. By the same token, none of the sociological theories given above seem to explain murder very well.

I mentioned earlier that murders are relatively easy for the police to solve. Why is this? It is because the large majority of murders are committed by people who know their victims personally. For that matter, the largest single category of murders happens within the family, especially one spouse murdering the other. Hence to solve a murder is not particularly difficult. The police need only look for someone who knew the victim and who had some motive to be especially angry with them. So if you are thinking about killing your husband or your wife, forget it; you will automatically be the number one suspect.

All this adds up to a picture in which crimes divide into quite different sorts. There are victimless crimes, very much created by social movements that define them as criminal; people who become labeled as criminal because of these sorts of offenses usually become involved in networks of other sorts of criminality as a result of the law-enforcement process. There are also property crimes, which have some relevance to the way in which individuals make their careers as criminals, but which would by no means disappear if laws stopped being enforced. And there are crimes of passion, which seem to be of a much more personal nature, and which do not seem to be related to any of the factors we have considered here.

Is there any perspective that encompasses all of this? Yes, I believe there is. But it is the most nonobvious of all, and one which does not resonate any too well in the hearts of either conservatives, liberals, or radicals. It is a perspective that declares that crime is a normal, and even necessary, feature of all societies.

THE SOCIAL NECESSITY OF CRIME

This perspective, like so many of the nonobvious ideas in sociology, traces back to Émile Durkheim. In this view, crime and its punishment are a basic part of the rituals that uphold any social structure. Suppose it is true that the process of punishing or reforming criminals is not very effective. The courts, the police, the parole system—none of these very effectively deter criminals from going on to a further life of crime. This would not surprise Durkheim very much. It can be argued that the social purpose of these punishments is not to have a real effect upon the criminal, but to enact a ritual for the benefit of society.

Recall that a ritual is a standardized, ceremonial behavior, carried out by a group of people. It involves a common emotion, and it creates a symbolic belief that binds people closer to the group. Carrying out rituals over and over again is what serves to keep the group tied together. Now in the case of punishing criminals, the group that is held together is not the criminals' group. It is the rest of society, the people who punish the criminals. The criminal is neither the beneficiary of the ritual nor a member of the group that enacts the ritual, but only the raw material out of which the ritual is made.

Picture a courtroom scene. A man is being charged with murder. The scene is theatrical in a stiffly traditional way. The judge sits up behind a high wooden desk, cloaked in a black robe, an aloof and authoritative figure symbolizing the law. The wood-paneled walls are lined with volumes of statutes and cases: the history of the law is there in gilt bindings. A railing marks off the area in front of the judge's bench, a kind of sacred space guarded by an armed bailiff, into which no one may enter without the judge's consent. To one side, the jury is cordoned off in another special space, the jury box. The accused prisoner is in another special place in the room, flanked by his defense lawyers and by more armed guards: the negative space of the prisoner's box into which no one would willingly tread.

The whole scene, in short, is ritualized, a tableau displaying the various parties to the enactment of justice. Witnesses are brought forward and sworn to take the proceedings in an especially solemn manner, incurring the risk of punishment upon themselves if they fail to do so. The attorneys for each side argue the case, following an elaborate etiquette, and attempting to stir up a collective sentiment among the jury members that will sway the verdict in their favor. And back behind the railing sits the public, both in person and in the intermediaries of the press.

It is this last group—the public—who are the true object of the ritual. The trial, ultimately, is staged for their benefit. A murderer is found guilty, or not; in either case, the law is personified, acted out, made into a living being. The public is impressed, once again, that the laws do exist, and that they are not to be violated. Especially when someone is found guilty of a serious crime, above all a spectacular murder, which draws the attention of the whole community, the ritual has a powerful emotional effect. That is when there is a maximal public focus on this ceremonial event and the widest participation in the collective emotion. For the dynamics of the ritual, it does not matter just what kind of emotion this is; it could be revulsion and disgust against a heinous act, or anger and the desire to punish, or on the contrary, sympathy for the accused in the awareness of mitigating circumstances. The important thing is that the emotion be a strong one, and that it be widely shared. It is this common emotional participation that draws the group together, and reestablishes it as a community.

The main object of a crime-punishment ritual, then, is not the criminal but the society at large. The trial reaffirms belief in the laws, and it creates the emotional bonds that tie the members of society together again. From this point of view, exactly how the criminal reacts to all this is irrelevant. The criminal is an outsider, an object of the ritual, not a member of it. He or she is the necessary material for this solidarity-producing machine, not the recipient of its benefits. It is the dramatics of the trial that counts, the moments when it is before the public eye. Afterwards, it may all come unravelled. The conviction may be reversed on appeal for some technical error. Criminals may go to an overcrowded prison where they make new criminal contacts and acquire a deeper commitment to the criminal role. Sooner than expected, the parole board may decide to relieve crowding in the prison by releasing them, and they are back out on parole and into the routine of police checks and parole officers and all the rest of an ongoing criminal career. If we look at the criminal justice system from the point of view of somehow doing something to deter the criminal, it appears ineffective, even absurd. It makes more sense once we realize that all the social pressure falls upon dramatizing the initiation of punishment, and that this is done to convince society at large of the validity of the rules, not necessarily to convince the criminal.

An even more paradoxical conclusion follows from this. Society needs crime, says Durkheim, if it is to survive; without crimes, there would be no punishment rituals. The rules could not be ceremonially acted out and would decay in the public consciousness. The moral sentiments that are aroused when the members of society feel a common outrage against some heinous violation would no longer be felt. If a society went too long without crimes and punishments, its own bonds would fade away and the group would fall apart.

For this reason, Durkheim explained, society is in the business of manufacturing crimes, if they do not already exist in sufficient abundance. Just what would count as a crime may vary a great deal, relative to what type of society it is. Even a society of saints would find things to make crimes out of: any little matters of falling off into less saintliness than the others would do. To put it another way, the saints, too, would have their central, especially sacred rules, and those who did not respect them as intensely as the others would be singled out for punishment rituals that served to dramatize and elevate the rules all the more.

How much of Durkheim's theory can we accept? Some of the way it is phrased, I would say, is inaccurate. Durkheim presents us with a functional argument: *if* society is to survive, *then* it must have crime. But there is no necessity that any particular kind of society must survive; hence there is no necessity that crime should exist for this purpose. Durkheim is better looked at as explaining a mechanism that *sometimes* is used: if certain rituals are carried out (in this case, punishment rituals), then social integration increases; if not, then there is less integration. Whether or not the mechanism will be used is another matter.

But if we shift our viewpoint slightly, we can see that there will be plenty of occasions when the mechanism will in fact be invoked. Society as a whole is only a concept, and hence "society" does not actually *do* anything. The real actors on the stage

are various individuals and groups. It is these groups that use
ritual punishments in order to increase their own feelings of solidarity and their own power to dominate other groups.

So we can say that concern about punishing criminals is an
aspect of the struggle among groups. It is a symbolic form of
politics. If you think about it, there is no strictly rational reason
why people should be concerned about crimes against other
people. Why should I care if someone else is robbed, murdered,
or raped? That is not a very moral or public-spirited thing to
say, but that is precisely the point: people have to feel some
moral involvement with a group for them to care about "the
crime problem." You could reply, of course, that everyone should
be worried about crimes against other people because it could
happen to you, too. Well, yes and no: about 1 percent of the
U.S. population is the victim of some sort of crime every year.
Objectively, your reasons for identifying with crime victims are
not very strong if your chance of being victimized is so low.

Some groups, it is true, have much higher victimization rates:
the poor, blacks, and the young. Teenagers, who commit the
most crimes, are also the most frequent victims: whereas well
below 1 percent of people over age fifty are subject to a crime of
theft or violence, as high as 15 percent of all teenagers have
something stolen from them each year, and about 6 percent are
subject to violence. Paradoxically, *it is precisely those people
who are least subject to crime who are most upset about the
crime problem.* Concern about crime, then, is largely a symbolic
issue. Those people who are most subject to it are the ones least
likely to raise an outcry about it.

The process, I suggest, is a political one; crime is a political
issue. Some politicians talk about it a great deal. Why should
they want to do so? Because the very idea of crime arouses
many people, especially if it can be invoked in an imaginative
way so that people identify with the victims of crime. The newspapers and mass media aid in this by vividly publishing those
particular crimes that have the most "human interest." But these
are the crimes in which the victim is the most *untypical,* i.e., a

senior citizen, or from the upper class or white population. This kind of selective dramatization of crime and its punishment (the courtroom scene) works as a Durkheimian ritual to mobilize the population—and incidentally, to help get certain politicians elected because of their strong leadership on the crime problem.

These rituals appeal the most to people who are already tightly integrated into dominant groups. The key audience consists of prosperous middle-aged or elderly people in suburbs and small towns, for example, who get a moral charge out of reading about the crime problem in the newspaper while sitting back in their easy chairs. These are the people whose own communities are organized with the greatest amount of ritual solidarity, and hence they are most susceptible to the moral appeal of punishing criminals who have victimized someone else. They are also the people who are most concerned to punish offenders on purely symbolic issues, such as drugs, gambling, or prostitution. These "crimes without victims" do not actually affect the people who are outraged by them at all. They are rather symbolic offenses against the ideals that the highly integrated, and hence highly moralistic, dominant groups consider to be the essence of righteousness. It is by getting upset about victimless crimes that these groups reassert their own status and their own feelings of righteousness. The very act of being outraged makes them feel their own membership in "respectable" society.

Punishment rituals hold society together in a certain sense: they hold together the structure of domination. They do this partly by mobilizing emotional support for politicians and the police. Above all, they increase the feelings of solidarity within the privileged classes and enable them to feel superior to those who do not follow their own ideals. Outrage about crime legitimates the social hierarchy. The society that is held together by the ritual punishment of crime is the stratified society.

In this sense, crime is built into the social structure. Whatever resources the dominant group uses for control will have corresponding crimes attached to them. Since there is an ongoing struggle among groups over domination, some groups will violate other groups' standards. And those individuals who are least integrated into any groups will pursue their own individual aims without regard for the morality held by others. Therefore, there is usually no shortage of actions that are offensive to many groups in a society. And these violations are to a certain extent welcome by the dominant groups. Crime gives them an occasion for putting on ceremonies of punishment that dramatize the moral feelings of the community, which bolsters their group domination.

This means that every type of society will have its own special crimes. What is constant in all societies is that somehow the laws will be set in such a way that crimes and punishments do occur. A tribal society has its taboos, the violation of which calls down ferocious punishment. The Puritans of the New England colonies, with all their intense moral pressures, believed in the crime of witchcraft. Capitalist societies have endless definitions of criminality relating to property. Socialist societies have their crimes as well, especially political crimes of disloyalty to the state, as well as the individualistic crimes of failing to participate whole-heartedly in the collective. The ritual perspective finds that all societies manufacture their own types of crime. It may be possible to shift from one type of crime to another, but not to do away with crime altogether.

Crime is not simply a matter of poverty and social disorganization, nor of particularly evil or biologically defective individuals. The labeling theory is closer to the truth, but the processes are much wider than merely social-psychological occurrences within the minds of offenders. Criminals are only part of a larger system, which encompasses the whole society.

THE LIMITS OF CRIME

If the whole social structure is producing crime, we might wonder if there is any limit to how much crime it produces. If crime helps hold society together, doesn't it follow, paradoxically, that the more crime there is the better integrated the society will be? Obviously, there must come a point at which the amount of crime is too great. There would be no one left to enforce the laws, and society would fall apart.

Nevertheless, this does not usually happen. If we look further into the matter, the reasons turn out to be not so much that the law-enforcement side effectively controls crime, but that crime tends to limit itself. Look at what happens when crime becomes more and more successful. Individual criminals can do only so much. They are much more effective at stealing, embezzling, or whatever if they are organized. Individual thieves give way to gangs, and gangs to organized crime syndicates. But notice, organized crime now becomes a little society of its own. It creates its own hierarchy, its own rules, and it attempts to enforce these rules upon its own members. Organized crime tends toward regularity and normalcy. It begins to deplore unnecessary violence and strife. The more successful it is, the more it approximates an ordinary business. The very success of crime, then, tends to make it more law-abiding and less criminal. The same thing can be seen historically.

At some points in history, political power consisted of little more than marauding gangs of warriors or robber barons that plundered whoever came their way. The very success of some of these well-armed criminals, if we may call them that, meant that they had to take more responsibility for maintaining social order around them. At a minimum, the violent gang of warriors had to maintain discipline among themselves if it was to operate effectively in plundering others. The more successful a robber-baron became, the more he turned into an enforcer of laws. The state arose from a type of criminality but was forced to create a morality just to survive.

If social life creates crime, then crime also tends to create its own antithesis. Crime tends to drive out crime. It is not so easy, after all, to be a successful criminal. If you start out today to be a thief, let us say, how do you go about it? In many ways it is like learning any other occupation. You need to learn the tricks of the trade: how to break into a house, how to open a locked car. You need to know where to acquire the proper tools: where to get guns, if you want to be an armed robber. And you need to learn how to dispose of the loot once you have stolen it; it doesn't do you much good to steal a lot of television sets and stereos if you have no way of selling them for cash. And the more expensive the stolen goods, the more difficult it is to dispose of them profitably. To realize very much when stealing jewelry or artwork, for example, one needs both special training in how to recognize objects of value and special connections for getting rid of them. Stolen cars, too, because of the elaborate regulations of licensing and serial numbers, can only be profitably gotten rid of by tying in with a smoothly functioning criminal organization.

Any new criminal starting out on a life of crime has a lot to learn and many connections to make. Most novice criminals cannot make it very far in the crime world for exactly the same sort of reasons that most people in legitimate business never make it to the level of corporation executive. The average robbery nets less than $100, which is not exactly a fast way to get rich. Crime is a competitive world, too, as soon as one goes into it seriously in order to make a good living from it. Part of this is a kind of market effect, a process of sheer supply and demand. The more stolen goods show up at the fence, the less will be paid for them. The more criminals involved in any particular racket, the less take there will be for any one of them. Established criminals have no reason to want to help just anyone who wants to learn the trade and acquire the necessary connections. Hence, many novice criminals are simply "flunked out"; there isn't enough room for them in the world of crime.

Perhaps it is for this reason that crime rates peak for the youth population between ages fifteen and eighteen, and drop off rapidly thereafter. Youths at this age are not seriously committed to crime; they do not know much about the criminal world. They don't have much money of their own, or very much sense of what one can do with money. Small robberies may seem like an easy way to get a few luxuries. Auto theft, for example, is especially high at this age. But teenagers have little sense of how to market a stolen car; they are more likely to joy-ride around in it for a while and then abandon it. Obviously one can't make much of a living out of this sort of thing. If the crime rate starts dropping off in the late teens, and reaches a fairly low level by the age of thirty, it is not so much because of the effectiveness of the law enforcement system but simply because most youthful criminals wash out of a career in crime. (Again, as I mentioned, most crimes are committed by males, and that is the occupational pattern to pay attention to here.) Crime simply doesn't bring in enough income for them, and they are forced to turn to something else to make their way in the adult world.

In the final analysis, the problem of crime, and its solution as well, is built much more deeply into the social structure than common sense would lead us to believe. Crime is so difficult to control because it is produced by large-scale social processes. The police, the courts, the prisons, the parole system are not very effective in counteracting criminality, and their very ineffectiveness seems foreordained by their largely ritualistic nature. Yet on the other side, crime has its own limitations. It works best the more it is organized, but the more organized it becomes, the more it becomes law-abiding and self-disciplining in its own ways. Individual criminals get squeezed out by the competitiveness of the world of crime itself, forced back into the world of ordinary society and its laws, whether they like it or not. Crime and society sway back and forth on this dialectic of opposing ironies.

5

LOVE AND PROPERTY

For a very long time the family and the relation between the sexes was one of the most taken-for-granted aspects of society. The obvious view has been that men and women have certain natural functions. Man's place is at work and in the public realm. Woman's place is at home, minding the kitchen and the children. The family is a natural division of labor between the sexes. Man is the breadwinner and defender, woman the homemaker and childrearer.

In the twentieth century women left the household in large numbers, but even then for a long time it was taken for granted that women at work would be subservient to men: they could work as a secretary, a nurse, a waitress, or a stewardess, serving a male boss or a male customer. A woman might be a school teacher of small children, but not a college professor, except in an all-female college. Even in the public realm, women were expected to carry over the same role that they had in the home, taking care of men and children.

This view has now come under attack. Once again, vigorous movement for sexual liberation is under way, and has begun to put pressure against some of the most obvious instances of job discrimination against women. At the same time, it is clear that the feminist movement has a long way to go in achieving its goal of equality between the sexes. Some women have begun to

119

make it into the higher realms of the professions, business, and
politics. But the vast majority of working women are still trapped
in sex-typed occupations like secretarial work and nursing, which
are not only relatively low-paying, but offer no chances of promotion into the higher, male-dominated spheres of their bosses.
The family, too, remains largely traditional in its operation, as
women are left with most of the household and childrearing re-
sponsibilities, even if they also have a job.

What is likely to happen in the future? The obvious view offers little guidance. On the one hand, if the old division of labor
between the sexes were absolutely natural, then no change
would be possible at all. The fact that *some* change has occurred
is inexplicable on this traditional view. A reactionary movement
has cropped up in some quarters in response to women's liberation. This movement tries to push women back in the confines
of the family and to reestablish all the old traditional sexual attitudes. But the very existence of the profamily, antifeminist
movement is itself a sign that something has gone wrong with
the traditional arrangement of things. If the old-fashioned family were so natural, it would not be necessary to force people
back into it.

On the other hand, there is a growing feeling that the family
itself may be on the way out. The birth rate has fallen off, so
that there are fewer children, and the divorce rate has climbed
to a very high level. How does this fit into the picture? Is it a
sign of social disorganization and approaching doom, as the traditionalists would have it? Or is it somehow connected with the
movement toward women's liberation?

Here sociological theory has an important nonobvious contribution to make. But once again, we must be selective. A good
deal of traditional sociology has only embellished a version of
the obvious view, seeing the family and traditional sex roles as
perfectly functional units in modern society. But there is another, much more sophisticated view of things. A branch of the
sociological tradition as far back as Friedrich Engels in the late
nineteenth century has helped us to understand that the family

and sexual relations are not just natural but exist as part of a system of stratification. The theory of sexual stratification is right now in the process of being developed, and there is a good deal of discussion over just how it works. But certain basic, and nonobvious, points can be made.

The guiding idea that I will follow here is that family relations are relations of property. This property is of several kinds: (1) property rights over human bodies, which we might call *erotic property;* (2) property rights regarding children—let us call this *generational property;* (3) property rights over goods held by the family—call this *household property.*

The family is made up of these three kinds of property. The way in which they mesh with the world of work, I contend, is a major determinant of sexual job discrimination. Once we can understand these forms of property, it becomes important to see that they are not static. Property systems, including sexual ones, are not natural and immutable forever. They are produced by certain social circumstances, and they change with those circumstances. If we understand these conditions, we can predict the rise and fall of various kinds of sexual stratification. The current type of family structure, and of sexual domination, has not existed forever, and it will not continue indefinitely into the future. If we wish to know how far women's liberation can proceed, and what conditions can make it possible, it is to a theory such as this that we must turn.

EROTIC PROPERTY

How can people be property? Except for slavery, which hardly exists anymore, people cannot be bought and sold. Human beings have no monetary value; we regard ourselves as beyond money. People are not things; they are ends in themselves. Hence, it would seem that people are not property, at least not in the modern world.

The mistake, though, is to think of property as a thing, and especially as a thing that can be bought and sold for money.

Property is not actually the thing itself, a physical object. Property is a social relationship, *a way in which people act toward things*. What does it mean, for instance, that a piece of land "belongs" to someone? It means that person can use it, live on it, go on it when he or she likes, and that other people must stay off unless they are given permission. If they don't, the owner can call the police or go to court to keep others off. Property is a relationship among people regarding things; it is some kind of enforceable agreement as to who can or cannot do what with certain things, and who will back others up in enforcing these actions. It is the society, that makes something property, and not some inviolable relationship between one individual and the soil.

This also implies that there can be all kinds of property systems, depending on just what kinds of rights society will enforce. In Sweden, for example, the right of private property does not extend to keeping the public off private land; strangers have the right to hike across anyone's fields or cut across anyone's yard, providing they do not disturb anything. In the United States, the sentiment of private property is a good deal stronger, but it is still backed up by the community, not by the individual. And the community reserves certain controls over what individuals can do with their property. They cannot build a garbage dump on a residential lot, for instance, and they can't keep the police off when searching for a fugitive. These laws are not immutable, of course; a society can set up any kind of property system it likes. Only *some* property systems allow for buying and selling by means of money. Some medieval aristocracies were not allowed to sell their land, and in many tribal societies property could be transferred only to certain kinfolk.

If property is a social relationship, then, rather than the thing itself, it makes sense to look at love and sex as forms of property. The key aspect of property is the right of possession, the right to keep someone else from possessing it, and the willingness of society to back up those rights. The very core of a marriage is property in just that sense.

What makes people married? It is not primarily the marriage vow, nor the civil or religious ceremony. A couple who live together and have sexual intercourse exclusively with each other are for all intents and purposes married. If this goes on for several years, in many places they are thereby legally married, as a "common law" marriage. On the other hand, a couple who are legally married but never have sexual intercourse is said not to have "consummated" the marriage. This is grounds for legal annulment, since the implicit terms of the marriage contract are not put into effect. In our society, marriage is a contract for exclusive rights to sexual access between two people. Socially speaking, they are exchanging their bodies as sexual property to each other.

This sexual property is the key to the family structure; it is the hinge on which everything else turns. Marriages are created by establishing the sexual tie. The old traditions of the wedding night and the honeymoon point directly to this fact. The more traditional the marriage, the more ceremony there was surrounding the first act of sexual intercourse. This went on whether or not people censored the fact that they were establishing a form of erotic property. Traditionally, before the legal reforms of recent decades, the only way one could get divorced was by proving adultery. This has been true virtually up to the present day in conservative, Catholic-dominated countries such as Italy. Why is adultery so crucial? Because it is a breaking of the central property right, exclusive sexual access.

Similarly, in traditional societies, heavy emphasis was placed upon the bride being a virgin at marriage. The husband's property rights over her body would have been sullied if she had had intercourse with another man. That these same societies tended not to regard male virginity at marriage as very important implies that the property system was much more one of males owning women's bodies than vice versa. I will come back to this.

The erotic property system is especially visible when we look at the points at which it is violated. There has long been a sort of unwritten law, which condoned spouses taking violent action when their sexual property was abused. A judge or jury usually would not convict a man of murder for killing his wife's lover, or even his wife, when he discovered her having an adulterous affair. Presumably, this should apply in reverse, too, but instances of wives getting away with killing their husbands or their lovers seem to have been less common—an example of sexist bias here, even in the right to kill. The notable thing is that such a killing is not usually regarded as a murder, and the killer is allowed to go free or given a light sentence. The custom of allowing a completely unpunished killing to take place in these circumstances has declined somewhat in contemporary times. Why this is so also reveals something about the sexual property system.

The practice of adultery-killing was strongest in places where marriage was regarded as most inviolate and divorces were least common. Why should this be so? Because this traditional marriage system meant that a woman would have only one sexual partner in her lifetime; her body was the exclusive sexual property of her husband. Such arrangements have usually had a rather sexist tone in that men were more likely to be allowed to have extramarital affairs or access to prostitutes; so, although a marriage was in principle unbreakable, the man had more opportunities for compensating for erotic and emotional incompatibility. With the rise of the divorce rate, though, in many communities it is generally expected that most people will have more than one marriage, and hence more than one sexual partner in their lifetime. For this reason, sexual property is no longer taken as such an absolute, something that if tarnished once is forever gone. This is not to say that sexual property no longer exists. But it has shifted into a different modality: one might say, from absolute long-term property to a series of short-term property arrangements. People still get angry about adultery, but the result is more likely to be a divorce instead of a violent death.

Laws and customs about violence tell us other things concerning erotic property. Virtually everywhere, a rape within a marriage is not a crime. According to the law in most countries, and all but a small number of American states, a man has the right of sexual access to his wife, and she cannot use the power of the state for protection against his forcing himself upon her. Implicitly, the marriage contract gives away the right of sexual resistance once and for all. The fact that the issue is now being raised, and that some places have made a crime out of marital rape, indicates the extent to which the sexual property system is being challenged today. But the resistance to such a legal change continues to be strong. To some extent it is balanced by the prevalent right to divorce that has emerged in recent decades, which makes it easier for a woman to escape from an undesirable husband.

All of this discussion seems to imply that marriage is simply a matter of sex, and that there is no affection, no love, involved. But this is certainly not so. Erotic relations are the key to the marriage contract, both legally and in the unwritten laws of customary belief. But this is by no means exclusive of emotional ties. In fact, the emotional ties now usually go along with the sexual ones. Love and sex, from a sociological viewpoint, are part of the same complex. At least this is so in the modern marriage system, which places a great deal of emphasis on an ideal expression of love. One might even refer to modern marriage as a ritual-love system of erotic property. In a certain sense, the erotic relations are deeper, and go back further. Marriage in traditional societies (as we shall see) placed little or no importance upon love, and concentrated instead on the control of erotic property and the other forms of property exchange involved in the main alliance. Modern marriage, though, has shifted into a form in which love is a crucial element in establishing a sexual tie.

There are several ways in which we can show that the emotions of love are tied to the erotic property system. For starters, look at the language of romance. Aside from "I love you," the most common sorts of love-expressions are phrases like: "Will you be mine?" "Take me," "I'm yours forever." Popular songs are full of this terminology, and so is the way people ordinarily converse about their loves, both among themselves and to other people. It is the language of property. "My," "mine," "his," "hers," "yours" are probably the most common words in love talk, even more than the word "love" itself.

All this possession-talk, moreover, refers simultaneously to affection and to sex. A lover possesses the other's body and affections at the same time. One is usually the symbol of the other. The man who says he loves a woman but will not have intercourse with her ("make love to her," in the telling phrase), either inside or outside a marriage tie, is certainly going to be doubted in his expression of affection. The same is of course true (perhaps even more so) the other way around, concerning the woman's behavior.

We can look at the same thing from the negative side. The kinds of things that make a lover jealous apply both to sexual behavior and to affections. A woman who professes to love a man but sleeps with someone else is more than likely to make him jealous, and at least to make him doubt whether she is sincere when she says she loves him. In the same way, she could make him jealous by sleeping with him but declaring that she loves someone else. People expect that love and sex will go together: at a minimum, they feel that truly strong love ties result naturally in sexual intercourse. Many people (though men more than women) will openly say that sex can be enjoyed without love, although this usually means that some degree of affection should be there. This seems to imply at least a short-term emotional tie, if not one of the "I'm yours forever" form.

The comparative study of jealousy gives a neat illustration of the social basis of emotions. Whom one feels jealous toward is relative to how sexual property is arranged. In our society, where erotically exclusive male-female pairs are the predominant form of sexual exchange, each partner is jealous of anyone who threatens to impose on the affections, or the genitals, of their partner. In polyandrous societies, however, the situation is quite different. This is a type of system, found for example in some of the mountain tribes of India and Tibet, in which a woman has several husbands. Usually it is a group of brothers who have the same wife. They are not jealous of each other, and all are expected to have a share in the woman's body and attentions. This does not mean such people are so broad-minded as to be incapable of jealousy. On the contrary, they can be quite jealous of outsiders who are not part of the polyandrous situation. Similarly, Eskimo men frequently share their wives, on a temporary basis, with visitors who come their way on long hunting expeditions. At the same time, Eskimo societies have had a very high incidence of fights and murders, often over possession of a woman. It makes a tremendous difference whether a guest is invited to share a woman (implicitly in return for some later reciprocity) or if he simply helps himself. Property, in short, is not given up when it is given away. In fact, the giving of a gift (in this case, a loan of a woman's body) reaffirms the sense of property, precisely because it makes clear to everyone involved that someone is doing something with *their* property and that they expect it to be received in a proper way.

These kinds of polyandrous or wife-lending situations actually are rather rare on the world scene. Somewhat more common are marriage systems in which a man has several wives. Such polygynous systems are especially prominent in tribal Africa. There, again, we find jealousy turned in quite different directions than in our own society. The various co-wives are usually not jealous of one another, although they may be jealous of outside women who are not part of the family situation. There is usually a chief wife, who has certain rights and powers over the other wives. In such a situation, a woman contemplating marriage may be more concerned about whether she will be moving into a family in which she gets on well with the co-wives than with how well she likes the husband himself.

This kind of anthropological comparison lets us see that the emotions we usually associate with sexual relations are variable, but not at all random. Just how much affection there is, and how much jealousy, and at whom it is directed, depends on the typical structure of sexual property relations. In our own society, erotic relationships are heavily imbued with romance, and emotions of affection and love are a crucial part of this. I am not saying that people fall in love because they feel they are supposed to. It is true that our popular culture tends to make people expect that this will happen, but the widespread experience of love is by no means simply the result of indoctrination by the media. Rather, it follows naturally from the type of negotiating that people must do in order to find a sexual partner in a situation of free individual bargaining.

Pretty much everyone today has to find their own partner. This involves a good deal of uncertainty. In the process of meeting various people to find out whether you like them, you may have many negative experiences as well. A man may pick out especially beautiful or sexy women only to find they are not interested in him. And why should they be? They are busy fending off all sorts of attentions, and unless this particular guy has something special to offer, they have no reason to notice him. A woman goes through similar processes on her side: setting her sights too high, or being stuck in a situation where she meets few desirable men, and so on. The sexual marketplace, in short, can often be an ordeal. At other times, things pick up: new partners appear, you find your attractiveness to others happens to be high, prospects look good. The roller coaster goes up again.

All this tends to make the sexual-bargaining process inherently emotion producing. It tends to generate feelings of anxiety, hope, fear, and also happiness and excitement. Hence, there is usually an emotional buildup when people find someone that they like, and joy if they find that this person, out of all the contacts they have tried, likes them too. Just how much a couple likes each other, even in these circumstances, may be a matter of degree. Each may still be eyeing the field, to see if there is someone they like better who might be attracted to them. A courtship thus can be somewhat uneasy for a while, until a couple finally settles down to a commitment to each other as the most favorable person they know. But this very uneasiness is what makes love affairs dramatic and arouses emotions. A couple that never goes through little reverses and potential breakups likely will not have as strong emotional feelings about each other as a couple that does.

I am suggesting, then, that the negotiating process itself tends to create strong emotions and that these feelings of tension and excitement, when they are finally resolved into a strong commitment to each other, are what turn into love. Moreover, the "language" by which a personal commitment is negotiated is likely to be to a large extent nonverbal: it is the language of sexual intimacy itself. A courtship is carried out not only by conversation but by a series of moves toward increasing physical intimacy. Touching, holding hands, kissing goodbye, necking, petting, intercourse—these are a typical progression, which sometimes may be drawn out at considerable length. The reason a couple does not usually go straight to the erotic climax is, in fact, because these various kinds of sexual contacts are heavily symbolic. They are not just pleasures in themselves. Sometimes they aren't necessarily even that: holding hands, for example, is not much of a physical pleasure, although it can be a highly emotional one. One could even suggest that many forms of much more intimate sexual contact, such as oral-genital contact, are also largely symbolic of a type of emotional relationship. They probably represent total intimacy, and perhaps total domination and submission, rather than simply physical pleasure.

The progression of physical intimacies, rather, is more like a ritual by which a man and woman indicate just how much commitment they have to each other. In general, they are bargaining their way into a tie, through various gradual steps that represent their tentativeness and the possibility that they might still pull back from the relationship. By the time the negotiation gets to full sexual intercourse, usually the couple has made some commitment to each other that involves a good deal of sexual exclusiveness, and along with this goes the emotion of love. This is, in fact, the way most modern marriages have been negotiated. By the time their personal movie has gotten to that final bedroom scene, they have brought themselves to being in love and are not far away from getting married. Or—to be realistic—at least they are entering that realm. The contemporary equivalent is living together, which is, from a sociological viewpoint, really identical to a legally backed marriage contract. Only a few years ago it was quite common for a woman to become pregnant by her boyfriend, as a way of forcing the final step of taking the marriage vow.

The emotion of love arises from the process of negotiating an exclusive and relatively permanent sexual contract among free individuals. It is a natural part of the drama that everyone goes through as they try to manage their own fate in a world where everyone else is simultaneously trying to do the same. From the ups and downs of the dating game come the ritualized establishing of the intense, private world of a new couple. It should not be surprising, then, that the emotion is strongest when the bond is first made, and during the period when it is confirmed as true and strong.

Here is when the actual behavior of the couple fits most closely the model for rituals that I first analyzed (chapter 2) in the case of religion. The ingredients of a ritual are all there, and in a very intense form. The couple is constantly in each other's presence and tends to exclude or ignore everyone else. Their love-talk and their kissing, hand-holding, and other erotic play have the patterned, repetitive form of ritual behavior. The emotions they bring to their encounters are intensified by being shared, just as any successful ritual revs up the feelings of the group. We can say, then, that lovers are carrying out a ritual that forms a very small, solidarity-group: a group of two, to be exact. This group has a very strong tie and very strong boundaries toward the outside.

And just as religious rituals create sacred objects and ideals, the love-ritual creates its own symbols that represent this intense tie. Some of these symbols are in the form of token objects, such as an engagement ring or some other keepsake or memento of the lovers. These are equivalent to a Bible or a crucifix sanctified by religious rituals, though a more exact analogy would be the private totems of one particular tribal clan. The world of lovers is more like a primitive religion than one of the encompassing world religions, like Christianity, since lovers are just one of a series of small private cults, which do not admit everybody. Certain ideas are made sacred, too, especially the idea that the lovers have of each other. It is no accident that lovers think of each other as absolutely wonderful, for that is precisely the kind of idealization that successful rituals produce. What is unique about the lovers' cult is only that the ideal is personified in the two individuals themselves.

The erotic property bond is thus formed by this kind of ritual. Hence it too, perhaps above all, is surrounded by ritual defenses. Any act of sexual intercourse or any erotic contact comes to symbolize the whole relationship. The negative side of this is that any sexual wanderings outside the relationship draw extremely angry reactions from the other partner. From a practical viewpoint, this cannot really be justified. A husband or wife might have intercourse with some outsider once, let us say, without actually disturbing their spouse's right to sexual access. The fact that merely a single instance of adultery can make the other spouse intensely jealous shows that the bond of erotic property is not simply a practical one but one upheld in a ritual fashion. Every act of intercourse, and for that matter even minor erotic acts like a kiss or even a glance, is symbolically charged. The realm of erotic property is like other really fundamental social ties: it is not rationally calculated in terms of an overall balance of costs and benefits but is enveloped in symbolism and driven by ritually produced emotions.

Erotic property and its counterpart, feelings of love and jealousy, are not the only sort of property relationships in a marriage. Moreover, their intensity does not stay at the peak hit when the relation bond was first being established. After a while, the excitement is gone, along with the anxiety and the contrasting joy. As a couple lives on into a marriage, the intensity of affection falls off and so does the frequency of sexual intercourse. They spend less time with one another and more time with other people. Hence the conditions for a strong ritual bond between them are weakened. But even as the intensity of erotic love falls, other ties frequently come in to take its place. I turn now to some of the others.

GENERATIONAL PROPERTY

In an important respect, children are property too. Parents have certain rights over them, and they act to defend those rights in the same way as they protect other kinds of property. Children are not, however, sexual property. All societies are very strict about this. The incest taboo within the nuclear family is virtually universal; sexual intercourse between parents and children, or among siblings, and sometimes among other relatives, too, is regarded with particularly strong revulsion. The incest taboo ought to be considered part of the generational property system; it is one of the principle *negative* rules as to what people *cannot* do with their generational property. (There are equivalent negative rules about physical property, too; zoning ordinances forbidding certain kinds of modifications of your house or land are instances of this.)

The incest taboo cannot simply be taken for granted, though. It is not a natural or instinctual revulsion; if so, no one would ever commit incest, whereas in fact the incest taboo is violated to a surprising extent. Rather, it is enforced above all from *outside* the family, by other people who look upon incest as improper and prosecute it as illegal. Why outsiders do this has largely to do with the general system of sexual bargaining that takes place in that society. People expect the children of other families to be available as sexual partners to outsiders, not to be monopolized within the family. It is possible to demonstrate this because different societies vary as to just what they count as incest, and these variations are tied to the kind of marriage system that prevails.

In some societies, like our own only a few generations ago, marriage with cousins was prohibited as incestuous, and people were expected to marry further afield. In many tribal societies, on the other hand, certain cousins are expected to marry each other whenever possible. This is because there is a system of regular alliances among families, and the continuous intermarriages of cousins (especially what are called "cross-cousins") is what keeps the families tied together generation by generation. Such examples, incidentally, prove that the reason for the incest taboo is not because people are concerned about possible genetic defects from inbreeding; societies practicing regular cousin marriage are obviously following the opposite of such a policy. Moreover, these same societies have incest rules that are in some respects much more extreme than our own; they prohibit large categories of people from marrying because they belong to the wrong lineage, even though we would consider them not very closely related biologically at all.

The reasons for the incest taboo are not biological but are part of the larger system of sexual property exchange. In our own society, wholesale alliances of families are no longer important, and our incest taboos have shrunk to the bare minimum that will still require children to leave their own family to find sexual partners in the larger marriage market.

The incest taboo, then, is a negative rule of the generational property system. It regulates what parents cannot do with their children, as well as what children are not allowed to do with each other. The positive aspects of generational property include a number of things. Parents have a certain physical property right over their children: the power to keep them in their houses, send them to school, and whatever else they wish to do with them. Parents have rights to direct their children's behavior in many respects: to determine how they dress; what religious training they are to be given, if any; whom they should associate with; and many other things. These rights are not necessarily very much enforced these days. We have come a long way from the Roman family in which the father could punish his children any way he wished, and even put them to death.

In general, the recent trend is toward reducing parents' control over children. Much of this follows from the loss of parental control over a crucial aspect of generational property, the power to determine whom their children would marry. (A vestige of this still existed just a few years ago, in the formality of a man asking his bride-to-be's father for her hand in marriage; and it is still common for the father to "give his daughter away" at the wedding ceremony.) Obviously, control over children's marriages extended generational property past the immediate offspring to a control in shaping subsequent generations of lineage. As family lineages have declined in importance, generational property has been shrinking, down to what applies only within the nuclear family during children's earlier years.

Generational property also has an economic aspect. Legally, children's incomes are the property of their parents, until they reach their majority. Again, this is a form of generational property that is not very much enforced these days. If anything, the opposite claim of children upon parents' income is much more prominent. But this only serves to tell us what changes have been happening in the recent family system. Not so long ago— and still today, in some very traditional families, such as where the whole family runs a store or a farm—children were expected to help support the family, either by working without pay in the family business or by going out and getting a job, and bringing their earnings back home.

Just as the erotic property system has been changing, the generational property system has been changing as well, and in a somewhat parallel direction. Another striking similarity between these two kinds of family property, though, is that both of them have a very prominent emotional side. And as in erotic property where spouses claim the right to each other's affections, parents have a right over their children's affection. Moreover, at the same time that the emotional relations among adults have become more central in the modern marriage, the affectional relations with children have come to displace the traditional emphasis on children as part of the farm economy or agents for carrying on the family name.

Again, we can see the strength of these emotional claims at the point where they are threatened by being broken. In contemporary divorces, usually the main point of contention is custody of the children. Parents fight over who will have physical possession, as well as over visitation rights. What is especially characteristic of the current situation is that both parents frequently are concerned to maintain maximal control over their children. It is no longer automatically assumed that children belong primarily to their mother. Fathers now want possession of their children much more than in the past. In effect, a certain aspect of generational property has become much more prominent, while other aspects decline. Emotional rights over children's affection has become central as the old economic and lineage concerns have declined. The situation has even given rise to a new species of "crime"—kidnappings in which one of the ex-spouses defies a court order giving custody to the other spouse and takes the children anyway. The fact that such cases are actually prosecuted, and are treated with so much emotion, shows how important emotional property rights over children have become.

Generational property, of course, cuts both ways. Parents have property rights over their children, but the reverse is also true. Children have a claim to a place in their parents' home, part of their income, and a certain amount of care. These rights, moreover, have apparently expanded in current society. Legally, these property obligations of parents to their kids come to an end at age eighteen, but there is considerable informal pressure to extend them beyond this point, as in paying for college expenses. The most important part of children's property claims upon their parents, however, used to be their inheritance. When much of the economy was run by family businesses, especially farms, this aspect of generational property was overwhelmingly important. It held the family together very tightly across the generations, but not necessarily in a way that was very affectionate.

Although the "obvious," conventional belief of today is that the family is nowhere nearly as tightly knit now as in the past, it is probably true that today's families place much more emphasis on emotional relations between parents and children, as well as between the spouses, than traditional ones did. The traditional family was held together because people had no choice: it was an economic unit, and people had to stick with it or risk starvation. This made for some rather cold-blooded attitudes toward family loyalty. Such families were strong but not usually very nice to live in. Today's families, for the most part, have relatively little material inheritance to pass on. People find jobs on their own and inherit little more than a few pieces of family furniture. Only among wealthy families has the old inheritance pattern remained important. For most other people there is little else left but the emotional ties. To be sure, these do not appear automatically. Many modern families do break up, whereas traditional ones probably would have stayed together even in the absence of affection just because the economic situation demanded it. But those modern families that do stay together do so more for emotional reasons than for external ones. In this respect, families are probably more strongly bonded than ever before.

HOUSEHOLD PROPERTY

It is not true, though, that the family is no longer an economic unit. It is just not a permanent economic unit based on the intergenerational transmission of property. From a certain point of view, it is an ongoing business, engaged in running a household. The business is by no means permanent; it can break apart much more easily than in the past. But while it exists, it is a cooperative enterprise for preparing food, doing cleaning, providing lodging, and caring for children. From an economic viewpoint, the family is a combination of hotel, restaurant, laundry, and baby-sitting agency.

In a traditional household, a great deal of the work would likely have been done by servants. Of course, only the higher social classes would have servants. A truly rich household would have a large number of them, but even a modest middle-class family would have at least a maid or a cook. What about the lower classes? To a fair degree, many of them had no household of their own: they were servants in someone else's household. This meant that family life was very skewed around social class patterns. It was largely the higher social classes who could afford to get married and set up a household of their own. Many of the working class men and women, living and working in someone else's house, would never have the opportunity to have families of their own.

One of the big changes in the modern family is the disappearance of this kind of large servant-based household. It is not that the upper class no longer exists, but its life-style has certainly become less dramatic and less grand; and the servant class has gradually faded away, certainly to a tiny fraction of what it once was.

Much of the servant class consisted of women who did the household chores in someone else's house. What remains of the servant class today is even more exclusively female; the butler and the valet have more or less disappeared, while the maid still comes to many upper-middle class homes today. For the most part, domestic labor has now fallen into the hands of wives. Insofar as the household is a place where work is done, it is primarily women who do it.

Officially and legally, the property of the household is now jointly held between husband and wife. In a divorce settlement, they have equal claims upon the goods accrued during their marriage; and if one spouse dies without a will, the other automatically inherits. But this is only taking the property as things. What about the things as they are actually used? A house, dishes, food, clothes—none of these are actually really usable just on their own. It takes a certain amount of labor to put them into operation. The house has to be kept clean, the clothes ironed, the beds made, the food bought and prepared and put on the table. In a common household economy, the husband may put in his labor

outside the household and bring home money, which he invests
in these various household materials. They are generally "raw
goods," and the wife puts in her labor in converting them into
consumable products. Moreover, this pattern tends to hold even
if the wife also works outside the household: she still takes care
of the home and the children, cooking breakfast before she goes
to work, cooking dinner when she comes back in the evening.

For this reason, the household economy can be described as
one of sex-based domination. Property is officially equal, but
only if one ignores the actual labor that turns it into usable, consumable goods. In the traditional case, where the husband alone
is working and bringing in money to invest in the household, we
have a household economy that is very much like a capitalist-
owned factory. The husband provides the raw capital; the wife
is the worker who has nothing to trade but her labor. Like any
other worker, she is forced by the pressures of staying alive on
the labor market to sell her labor to someone who can afford to
buy it; only in this case she sells it (or rather barters it) in a
household rather than a factory. But her labor is essential; the
husband/capitalist cannot transform his raw materials into usable
goods without it.

Of course, we can think of various differences between the
two situations: the factory worker does not end up inheriting the
factory; and the worker does not usually have sexual intercourse
with the owner, bear his children, share his social status, or
express any love and affection for him. Leaving these things
aside, though, recent Marxist-oriented feminist writers have argued that the household really is a capitalist institution. It is not
only capitalist in its inner workings but is part of the larger capitalist system of the society. What women's work in the home
does for the larger capitalist economy is to *reproduce the labor
force.* All the cooking, cleaning, shopping, child-care, and even
the emotional affection given to husbands serves to keep the extrafamilial male labor force ready to go to work the next day.
Labor is a crucial aspect of the capitalist economy, but the capitalists themselves do not see to its everyday maintenance. This

is left to the hidden economy of the household, where women do this essential work of keeping the capitalist system going.

The inference that is sometimes drawn from this is that women do not have a distinctive grievance vis-à-vis men; their grievance is really with the capitalist system. It may be true that the male working class is overtly more sexist in the way it treats women than the male middle or upper class is, but the overall picture throughout the society is one in which women do the household work for the sake of the capitalist system in general. It follows that women's real ally should be the working class (which they are really a part of); if they joined together in overthrowing capitalism, presumably women's subjugation in household labor would disappear too.

Short of some long-term revolution, at any rate, this sort of argument has various implications for reforming the system of household labor. It has been argued that wives should be paid salaries for their work, that there should be a minimum wage, and that they should be eligible for social security benefits. Alternatively, household labor should be socialized. Child-care can be taken over by a collective, extrafamilial child care center. Similarly, cleaning, laundry, food preparation can all be shifted to outside workers instead of being done by the wife in the home.

Interestingly enough, the latter pattern does seem to be emerging already. By and large it is not emerging in a socialized form, although public child care facilities are becoming more common. Much of the rest is provided by private business: fast food chains, prepared foods, cleaning services, and the like. To a considerable extent women now are in the paid labor force themselves, and they make use of other people to help take care of their children and their household economy. This is only partial, to be sure; as long as women are not paid as much as men for their outside work, the family is less likely to be able to afford to completely make up these family services with paid outside labor. Full-scale sexual equality in the future might well bring about this transformation of the household.

Where the Marxian model is weak, I would claim, is in its direction of causality. The current male-dominated household economy was not originally created by the rise of capitalism. We do not really know that shifting to a socialist economy would automatically eliminate sexual stratification. The experience of the Soviet bloc of socialist societies suggests that it would not. The underlying theoretical problem is that the Marxian model catches only one of the three kinds of property within the family: it concentrates on household property and ignores erotic and generational property. But these are the reasons why, as I noted a little earlier, the household is not quite like a factory. The sexual and emotional sides of the family enterprise are just what makes it different from a purely capitalist business: and these are the reasons, too, why a housewife inherits her place of work if its provider dies, but a factory worker does not. A man in marrying does not just acquire a household servant, although there is that aspect of it too.

In the realm of household labor and household property, changes have taken place not because women have waited for a socialist revolution but because they have pushed for a feminist one. To the extent that women have moved into the better-paying labor force, they have begun to change the household work situation. Husbands now make more contributions to caring for children and helping with the housework. Generally speaking, the relative power of women vis-à-vis their husbands is tied to how much money she makes relative to him. Women who earn more than their husbands are much more powerful at home than those who earn less. In this sense, as well as in others, the more successful women are in overcoming sexual discrimination in the larger society, the less inequality there is at home as well.

Still, one might wonder in a traditional frame of mind: why would a man put up with this? Wouldn't he rather marry a traditional woman, who does not work or at least earns less than he, so that he can dominate the household in the old-fashioned way? The answer, by and large, seems to be no. For one reason, a family with two significant incomes is much wealthier than a family with only one. In fact, the major way that people now can achieve a relatively luxurious upper-middle class life-style is for both husband and wife to be working at fairly good jobs. A highly paid wife has become a very big advantage for most men. In the marriage market that is now emerging, it is no longer just the ambitious women who are seeking out potential doctors or business executives to marry; a woman's own success is becoming part of her attractiveness.

THE RISE OF THE SEXUAL MARKETPLACE AND THE LOVE REVOLUTION

All of the three types of property that we have discussed go together in the family. It is hard to separate them, e.g., having children from having intercourse or living together erotically from maintaining a joint household. Presumably a joint household could be created without the erotic tie: two people could live together (irrespective of what their sexes might be), making a deal to share all their incomes and the household expenses and duties. But this would not very likely be sanctioned by a legal contract, with rules of inheritance; and it would not likely take the form of one person—always a female—doing all the household work, while the other—always a male—works only outside.

These patterns come from the tying together of all the different property systems in marriage. As we've seen, the core of a marriage is the erotic property contract, and all the rest is brought in around it. Now why should this be so? Why should a particular male-dominated version of this have come into existence, and what forces can change it into a more egalitarian condition? It is easiest to see the dynamics of this problem by making a series of comparisons.

There have been many different family systems throughout history. Many of these, especially in tribal societies, have been quite complex and very different from our own. Some have been matrilineal, others patrilineal: reckoning family descent and inheritance through mothers or fathers, respectively. They have also varied in determining where a couple lives: with its mother's kin (matrilocal) or father's kin (patrilocal). There have been many other combinations and ramifications. Our own marriage system, in these terms, is generally neolocal—the couple establishes a new household of its own—and bilineal—in the sense that inheritance takes place through both sides of the family, although usually the family name is still inherited patrilineally. (Feminists have sometimes made a point of shifting to a truly bilineal naming system: naming their children "Smith-Jones" instead of merely "Smith.")

There is no need to go through the history of family systems as these various tribal types gave way to the patrilineal/patrilocal, class-based households of the ancient and medieval civilizations. The major shift that concerns us is relatively recent, taking place within the last few hundred years. This was the shift from a marriage system in which the family determined the choice of marriage partners to the current system in which individuals negotiate for their own mates. Formerly whole families made alliances; the family patriarch worked out a deal whereby erotic property was exchanged in order to carry on economic holdings or consolidate political positions. This broke down when the economy and the state became organized in much larger bureaucratic entities, which no longer had much need for the family. Individuals were now left on their own, to negotiate their own ties, on an open marriage market. Each person now had to find a partner on their own, using whatever resources they might have: their own wealth or job prospects, their cultural background, their connections, good looks, personality, or whatever. The round of courtship goes on until each individual finds another who more or less matches what they personally have to offer, in relation to what they find they can get, and then a deal is struck.

This sounds mercenary, but in fact it is this wide-open market that is responsible for our modern-day ideal of love. The premodern arranged marriages were overtly much more mercenary than anything we have today. Married couples were not expected to have much personal attraction for each other, or even to have any say in the contract. This was obviously even more true in a tribal kinship system in which people were required to marry their cross-cousins. It is not that love did not exist in traditional societies, but it was not regarded as very important. Love might make a pretty story about a shepherd and a nymph, but it had nothing to do with the realities of marriage. Even the medieval troubadours, who created love stories about knights and ladies, dissociated these affairs from marriages by making it always the devotion of a knight to a lady who was already married to someone else. This is a reason why, in the stories at least, the love never had anything to do with sex and was a purely one-sided devotion on the part of the knight only.

The reality of this period was that individuals were just pawns in family marriage games. Their sentiments counted for little, and hence love relations in the modern sense rarely existed. Nor is this surprising if you view it in light of the theories regarding religion and ritual presented earlier (chapter 2) which explain how the density of human interaction affects what people hold to be most sacred. In these societies in which everything took place inside a tightly knit family group, moral sentiments were tied entirely to the group's identity. The cult of the individual is the creation of a much more recent social structure, in which each individual is exposed to their own particular mesh of contacts. It is for this structural reason that individual persons had very few rights in a traditional society; they thought of themselves, and of everyone else, basically as the member of some group. A love bond between one particular person and another, under this circumstance, was just not in the cards.

The big shift came when this family-alliance system was broken up by the individual marriage market. We might call this the Victorian Revolution, because it is best characterized by the attitudes about love and sex that prevailed during the mid-nineteenth century (although in fact the roots of this revolution go back into the previous century or so). In one respect, this was the love revolution; it meant that individuals were now allowed to marry for love, instead of by family pressure. Love was henceforth not only allowed: it became more or less expected. And, in fact, love relationships did begin to spring up, and quite widely, where hardly any had existed before.

Yet hand in hand with this came the rise of a highly Puritanical attitude about sex. Traditional societies, despite their very strong religious beliefs, were not particularly squeamish about sex. For them a marriage, since it did not involve love, was primarily about sex, as well as other kinds of property. Men in particular were not much restricted from taking sexual gratification where they wanted it. Concubines and mistresses were widely accepted, even sometimes given an official status in an aristocratic family. Children born out of wedlock were very common and were not looked upon with any sort of disgrace. To be the king's bastard son was not as good as being his legitimate son, since a bastard couldn't inherit the throne, but he was still a very favored person and would wear his illegitimate lineage proudly.

All this was swept away in the Victorian Revolution, or at least driven underground. A child born out of wedlock became a scandal, and the mother in particular was made a social outcast. An effort was made, for the first time, to suppress prostitution. Men's extramarital affairs became frowned upon (although they did not exactly cease). All sexual relations were supposed to be confined to the marriage. At the same time marriage became highly idealized; the erotic element was no longer to be mentioned. A man and a woman were supposed to marry for pure love alone, a sentiment felt on both sides and excluding any impure considerations. Mention of anything else, above all of sex, became socially taboo. The older linguistic expressions for sex, genitals, and bodily functions generally became replaced by a set of polite euphemisms.

It is apparent that the nature of the marriage bond had shifted and that it had become ritualized in a new way. Both the new prudishness and the new idealization of love were part of the same process. The taboo against direct mention of sex, and the scandals about any sexual violations, were the negative part of the ritual: they comprised the barrier against impurities that typically surrounds any sacred object. The positive, sacred side of the ritual, of course, was the ideal of love itself—more particularly, the ideal of pure love as the key to marriage.

As we've already seen, feelings of love really do arise out of the way in which individual courtship bargaining takes place. From the point of view of the way rituals work, this system produces just the right conditions for generating the love tie. It isolates two persons into a small group, puts them constantly in each other's presence, excludes outsiders from their intimate doings, matches them by a shared emotional level. The result is that their couplehood itself becomes a little sacred cult, and the words about "love," which they pass back and forth, become the symbols representing the group. Love is a kind of private mini-religion, in which the couple is the object of its members' veneration.

From a structural viewpoint, the love bond is actually the sentiment of erotic property bonding. The Victorian Revolution, even though it made people puritanical about sex, was actually a shift in which sex became much more central in the marriage tie than ever before. The proportional importance of the three kinds of property in a family had changed a great deal. Generational property in the form of family inheritance had dropped enormously, and no longer determined the choice of the marriage partner. This left erotic and household property, which were provided by the individuals themselves, and constituted the resources around which the marriage would be negotiated.

But in this historical period, these two resources were distributed very unequally between the sexes. The income to support a household was almost exclusively in the hands of the man, since extreme sexual discrimination in the labor market made it almost impossible for a woman to support herself except at very low-paying jobs. This discrimination was a result of the position of women in the preceding, traditional household, in

which they were either confined indoors as family property
for marriage alliances or worked only as servants. Now women
were free to choose their own lives. But in the absence of economic alternatives, any woman who wanted a decent middle-
class standard of living had to get married.

In effect, the marriage deal had now become a trade of erotic
property for household property. It was imperative for women
to try to confine sex as much as possible to marriage. For this
reason, premarital and extramarital sex now became scandalous.
Women tried to enforce this sexual standard upon men as well as
upon each other. Puritanism in behavior and prudishness in language were enforced to an unprecedented degree. And it worked.
During the Victorian Revolution women actually acquired at
least one source of power they had not had before: the power to
withhold their bodies from men as sexual objects. The marriage
market was open to everyone, and this also meant that everyone
had the right to refuse any particular exchange. Insofar as
women could maintain a more or less united front on the issue
of confining sex to marriage, men would have nowhere else to
go and would have to accept marriage on women's terms.

The ideal of marriage for love and the restraints of Victorian
prudishness about sex fitted together as part of this strategy.
Both were part of the struggle of women to gain some control
over their lives and raise their status in society. The ideal of pure
love was in a certain sense an ideology, hiding the erotic property deal that still lay very much at the heart of marriage. Actually, it pointed very explicitly to what it seemed to conceal, more
or less in the same way that Victorian clothing styles drew attention to the feminine figure by wrapping layers of covering
around the hips and making the glimpse of an ankle about as
erotic an experience for a man as a high slit skirt is today.

The Victorian Revolution turned out to be a success. Men
became more dependent upon their wives for sexual and emotional satisfaction. The love ideal and the puritanical restrictive-
ness could only be lived up to to a certain extent, of course. But
that degree was enough to cause a considerable rise in the status

of women. The Victorian Revolution was the first major phase of women's liberation.

From another viewpoint, however, the Victorian Revolution was also a dead end. It confined a woman's career to making a good marriage. The very idealization of woman as a pure crea-ture whom a man would love and marry and honor as the mother of his children and keeper of his home, helped maintain a sharp barrier between male and female. Males had the world of work outside, women had the marriage market and the family. The more the woman and her role in the family was ideal-ized, the harder it was for women to move out of it and achieve any kind of economic resources on her own.

In the twentieth century, there has been another revolution in women's status. It began slowly, as women gradually began to infiltrate into the white-collar labor force, and has picked up steam in the last few years, as women have begun to make a push into the better-paying professions and managerial ranks. This second revolution has simultaneously been a revolution in the structure of the family. The two kinds of shifts—occupational and familial—occur together. Each change has gradually fed the other, making possible more and more movement away from the Victorian pattern of household and erotic property.

What is happening is that women are becoming less depen-dent on the family for their economic fortunes. Every improve-ment in women's job opportunities has meant that women have depended less upon husbands for their incomes. The increase in divorce rates, the tendency for people to wait longer before get-ting married, the trend of having fewer children—all of these are connected to the greater ability of women to support themselves.

This has also affected the way in which erotic relations are negotiated. It has become much less important for women to confine sex to marriage. Premarital affairs are much more ac-ceptable now. A series of different sexual partners, in official or unofficial marriages (including living together), is compatible with this deemphasis upon a single, once-and-for-all tie in which a woman attaches herself permanently to one man and his income. For the same reason, women have become much less puritanical about their use of language. It is no longer important to spiritualize sex and to surround it by linguistic taboos. This is most true among women who are the most successful occupationally. For such women, erotic dealings and the marriage market itself are matters that they can approach much more casually, without a sense of irrevocable choice. Their whole lifetime no longer hangs upon it.

THE FUTURE OF THE FAMILY

What can we expect of the future? Will the family simply fade away into a series of sexual liaisons or perhaps some kind of open marriage with multiple sexual partners? Or on the contrary, have things already gone too far, and will a profamily backlash reestablish traditional sex roles and restrictions?

The answer to both questions is more than likely, no. The individual-based marriage market still exists and is likely to continue to do so into the foreseeable future. Its forms have changed somewhat as women have acquired more economic resources, but the main outcome is still that men and women negotiate an exclusive personal bond, with a fairly strong intention of making it last. Sex is much more open and explicit, but the importance of love is just as strong. And this too is likely to continue, because both sex and love are part of the same process of negotiation. Dispensing with marriage ceremonies actually makes no difference in the structure since living together is the essence of marriage in any case. All it does is to imply that a formal announcement to family and friends is no longer important; a living-together "marriage" is a completely privatized form of the arrangement.

It would be a major change, to be sure, if open marriages became widespread. This is an agreement in which both partners allow the other to have as many other sexual partners as they wish. This really would be a change since it would eliminate exclusive sexual property, which is the key to family structure in both official and unofficial, long-term and short-term forms. The existing process of falling in love follows from that exclusiveness as well. If open marriages were to become common, then we really would have an entirely new form of family organization.

But open marriages do not seem to be catching on widely. There is a structural reason why they are not usually successful. What seems to happen, according to sociological observations that have been made, is that a couple who have an open marriage tend to get into a competition. Just as in a more typical family the relative power of husband and wife is influenced by how much money each one makes, in an open marriage the relative power of man and woman depends on how many outside sexual partners each one has. It becomes a competition over who is sexually more desirable. Usually the woman wins the competition because a woman looking for sexual partners in our society today will have more ready takers than a man will. The result tends to be that after a while the man starts to feel he is losing out and that his partner is getting more out of the open marriage than he is. Paradoxically, although the man more likely raised the idea of an open marriage in the first place, he is also more likely to want to end it. In any case, open marriages are structurally unstable. Either the couple ends the experiment and returns to a more exclusive arrangement or the marriage falls apart and becomes an ordinary divorce.

Greater openness about sex, then, and less regard for the formalities of marriage do not mean that exclusive couple bonds are no longer important. The increase of premarital sex, for example, does not mean that anyone will sleep with just anyone. There is still a process of picking and choosing, and hence a tendency to pair off with someone else who stands about the same place in the sexual marketplace. We may not always call these arrangements "marriages," but that is essentially what they are. Even a high divorce rate—which may actually be a good deal higher than officially stated if we include the making and breaking up of informal marriage arrangements—does not mean marriages are on their way out. On the contrary, one could say that marriages are even more popular now since everyone has more of them than before.

It is true that this situation has been the subject of much controversy, and that a very explicit reaction has arisen to the greater sexual openness and the changes in family forms of today. There is now a publicly very vocal profamily movement, which is also usually antiabortion, antierotic, and antifeminist.

Nevertheless, I think that this movement is attacking issues that are largely symbolic. The traditional-family backlash is setting itself against the major structural trends of modern times. Consider the antiabortion issue. The issue has arisen, rather suddenly, because official government policy in the United States finally came to recognize what had been going on unofficially for a long time: there were large numbers of unwanted pregnancies and hence large numbers of illegal abortions. Legalizing abortion was a way of attempting to improve the safety of the women involved. For a long time the dangerous conditions under which women had these illegal abortions were never discussed; an abortion (and its usual predecessor, an illegitimate pregnancy) was a scandal that everyone hushed up. Once it was brought out into the open, the women's movement could make its point and get some reforms made. But the same publicity also allowed opposition to gather as well.

Militant opposition to abortion dates from the U.S. Supreme Court decision to decriminalize abortion in 1973. The antiabortion movement came on the scene as a backlash against one of the early successes of the modern women's movement. It is a symbolic crusade like some of the other movements in the past (discussed in the previous chapter), which have fought to create new categories of crime (or in this case, revive an old category of crime).

We may look at this from the point of view of the sociological theory of ritual solidarity. The antiabortion issue is seen by its proponents as entirely a moral issue. Clearly the people involved in it have nothing to gain from it personally; even vicariously, they are not identifying themselves as being like an unformed two- or three-month fetus. (This is even more obvious in the case of people who oppose birth control in general, as well as abortion, especially in Third World countries; they are thinking of the fetus in the abstract, rather than sympathizing with the fate of real children born into some poverty-stricken or even starving population.) It is not real children, and certainly not real women, who are the object of sympathy. The moral issue is a pure end in itself. If the issue is a symbolic one, then, what is the symbolism about?

The theory of ritual solidarity provides the answer. Emotional issues serve to bring a group together, especially when there is some outside group of evil-doers (in this case women who have abortions) to be castigated. The very fact that abortions were made legal provided a rallying point for a group that was beginning to feel rather in need of some new solidarity and a moral jolt to bolster their falling sense of status. The recent success of the women's movement has been especially threatening, not just to men—who as we have seen, often benefit from improvements in their wives' careers—but to traditional nonworking housewives. Such women, who have no preparation and no opportunities for making careers of their own, are stuck with the traditional family role. It may cast them in the role of limited, second-class citizens, but it is the best they have. The ideas and styles of the newer sexually egalitarian world created by more liberated women makes them feel doubly uncomfortable. On one count, they are uncomfortable because the more liberated women have acquired power, money, and personal status that they lack. On a second count, the ideals of women's liberation threaten what psychological defenses housewives once had by pointing out their second-class citizenship, which was once veiled by the glorification of the wife-and-mother ideology. There is a good deal of hurt beneath the surface of such traditionalists who are unable to move into the newer world.

It is these people who are especially attracted to symbolic crusades to restore the old order of sex roles. The movement consists of a series of ritual gatherings, like political meetings, which create emotional energy for those who belong. The "right-to-life" they are concerned about, beneath the ideals they officially invoke, is really the effort to breathe some life into their own badly depleted social status.

If such a movement were to succeed, of course, it would actually raise the status of its members. They would be a moral elite, like the old New England Puritans who burned witches at the stake, dominating the evil people whom they persecute. Such symbolic crusades have sometimes succeeded for a while in the past, like the rural Protestants who succeeded in imposing prohibition of alcohol from 1919 to 1933. But in the long run, I think, it is almost certain that the antiabortion movement will fail. Its practical consequence runs up against one of the main features of the current family situation. This is the decline in the birth rate, which has occurred in all societies around the world in recent decades. Abortion is a major part of birth control, running at the rate of well over 1 million per year in the United States. There are about 300 legal abortions for every 1,000 births, which means that if abortions actually ceased the birth rate would jump by 30 percent. This in fact would not actually occur if abortions were made illegal again. We would simply be back in the situation where large numbers of women would have dangerous illegal abortions. These women simply could not afford to have unwanted children; they would acquire abortions whether legal or not. Abortion is the last and strongest line of defense against unwanted childbirths, and hence is a fundamental aspect of birth control.

The underlying structural fact is that birth control has become an essential part of modern family structure. Birth control is essential for women who want to have any sort of career, for an uncontrolled succession of children would be the one thing that would tie them to the home. To overturn birth control it would be necessary to overturn the entire thrust of the modern women's revolution. Birth control, moreover, is economically buttressed. Childrearing is expensive, and has become increasingly so as education, housing, and child-care costs have gone up out of proportion to income. At the same time, the economic value of children has virtually disappeared, as they bring in no money to the family budget and provide no services to a modern household. A family now can usually afford to raise a large number of children only if both parents are working, which is also the very thing that prevents them from having many children. Zero population growth is no longer a project for the future. It is an actuality now. The improved occupational position of women is likely to keep it so.

More generally, the movement to restore the traditional, male-dominated family and the totally domesticated woman has very little chance of success. To restore the traditional Victorian family and the old puritanical pattern of courtship would require that the occupational trends of the twentieth century be completely reversed.

The only antifeminist strategy that could be truly effective would be not simply to oppose equal rights legislation but to positively ban women from holding any of the better paying jobs. What antifeminists need is legislation that actually *requires* discriminatory pay and institutes complete occupational segregation for men and women. This of course would be next to impossible, barring some political revolution toward an extremely authoritarian and conservative society, like the Fascist revolutions in Germany and Italy in the 1920s and 1930s. But short of this, the clock cannot be turned back. Too many women already have begun to make it into careers that are attractive enough to them so that they will no longer play the traditional marriage game of trading puritanically guarded sex in exchange for a husband's income.

By no means have women achieved economic and occupational equality with men; there is still a long way to go. But feminist mobilization has gone far enough that its footholds are not likely to be given up. In recent years, women have begun to exceed men proportionately in attaining higher education, and this foreshadows an ever greater commitment by women to making it into the better-paying job market. This trend cannot be turned back, short of some kind of totalitarian reaction. But the more the occupational situation shifts toward sexual equality, the more firmly the newer type of marriage market will take hold. The future of the family is more than likely to be on the side of the feminist revolution.

6

CAN SOCIOLOGY CREATE AN ARTIFICIAL INTELLIGENCE?

For the past few hundred years, people have been dreaming of creating a machine that can think. When modern science began to discover the principles of physics and chemistry, it occurred to some thinkers that the human body too might be constructed along the lines of a machine. Medical and biological discoveries of the physiological processes that regulate life made this seem even more plausible. Soon after it was discovered that nerves transmit electrical impulses, Mary Wollstonecraft Shelley wrote *Frankenstein*, in which a scientist brings a body to life with bolts of electricity.

We all know how that turned out! And the subsequent history of efforts to build an artificial human being has involved similar frustrations. When computers began to be invented in the middle of the twentieth century, the hope was that we would now understand how to make the high-speed electronic circuits that would truly model the human brain. Forty years later, the main thing we have learned is how incredibly difficult it is to mimic a real human being. Still, the dream persists. Sci-fi movies depict robots, sometimes shaped like a human body with shiny metal arms and legs, that not only speak and think but have real personalities, usually comic ones. The late twentieth century is already the age of science fiction coming true; the 21st century will surely take us into that orbit. Will a humanly created artificial intelligence be part of that future, or is it a foolish dream that will never come about? I want to suggest that if a real artificial intelligence (AI) is going to be built, sociologists will have to play a major part in it. The limits on computer models so far have resulted from the fact that they represent intelligence as if it were a free-standing individual mind. But human thinking is basically social. Not only that; a successful AI is going to have to be emotional! We have made a mistake in trying to make it too rational, too much of a super-intelligence, without the more essential human qualities. This may sound paradoxical, but I will try to show you that research in micro-sociology—studies of how people interact with each other in face-to-face situations—shows the emotional processes that keep up social contact and guide our thoughts along certain channels. If a computer intelligence is going to be able to do what a human can do, it will have to be a computer with emotions.

EXPERT SYSTEMS AND THE LIMITS OF COMPUTING

When computers were first invented after World War II, there was an effort to build what was called a "general problem solver." This was to be a computer that could do anything. Instead of being programmed merely to do one particular task (such as compute statistics), the general problem solver would be able to handle any problem that came along. In other words, it would act more like a real human thinker: analyzing what the problem is, figuring out what is needed to solve it, working it up until the solution appears. But this proved to be too difficult for computers. It wasn't just a matter of memory capacity; computers have gotten enormously bigger and faster over the years. But the difficulty with the general problem solver was that humans can think in a manner that includes so many more dimensions than merely making computations from existing formulas. Computer scientists came away with new respect for the complexity and power of the neural network that makes up the human brain, and gave up on building a general problem solver.

Instead, they turned to creating computer programs that are highly specific. Instead of solving all tasks, these programs are now tailored to know as much as possible about one specific area. These are *expert systems*. To create one, it is necessary to go about solving certain kinds of problems. Supposing you wanted a computer to make medical diagnoses of a certain disease; first you interview a group of doctors about the steps they go through in making a diagnosis. An "expert system" sounds sophisticated—after all it is an expert!—but in fact it is nothing but an electronic file cabinet. It arranges information in a branching tree, starting from introductory questions and leading to more specific ones. What are your symptoms? Is your temperature elevated? If yes, then we ask: is your throat sore? If yes again: is your throat red? Does it have a white coating? If no to one of the above, we ask a different line of questions: pain in the sinus regions? runny nose? are you under strain at work or school? Finally the computer "expert" has a combination of answers and reads out its solution: take two aspirins, drink plenty of fluids, and drop off the insurance form with the receptionist on your way out.

An expert system is very far from thinking like a full-fledged human being. It only stores information that has been put into it by human beings. It is only as good as the experts it was modelled on, and indeed only as good as the computer engineer at getting those experts to describe what it is they do when they make their diagnoses. The expert system doesn't come up with new ideas; and it doesn't know how to deal with exceptions. It is nothing but a file cabinet with a program to go through it in a certain order.

For these reasons, critics have argued that computers have intrinsic limits, and that they will never be able to think like real human beings. A computer may be able to calculate very rapidly and may store huge amounts of information. But it is only as good as the information that is put into it. As the saying goes, "Garbage In, Garbage Out"—the quality of the input determines the quality of the output. Computers are rigid; in some ways they are like very stupid people, who keep on making the same mistakes over and over again. If a computer makes a mistake in calculation, it doesn't have the "good sense" to correct it, unless a human operator specifically puts in a check for what is a reasonable range of outcomes. That is why computers always need their human baby-sitters. Even the new approaches that redesign the hardware into a network of computers working in parallel have not been able to overcome this problem. If the ideal is to have an artificial intelligence that can think like an autonomous human being, then it looks like computers will always be our infant protégés: they are like mental giants with the feet of little babies, who always need a nurse to care for them and keep them out of trouble.

SOCIOLOGY'S CONTRIBUTION TO A
TRULY HUMAN INTELLIGENCE

Why should we expect that sociology could help get around these problems? The most important reason is that thinking is fundamentally social. Sociologists since the time of Emile Durkheim, Charles H. Cooley, and George Herbert Mead have developed theories of the social basis of the human mind. We have already met some aspects of Durkheim's theory in chapters 1 and 2. Here we are going to put it to work, along with some of the ideas of Cooley and Mead, and the more recent microsociological researchers who have followed up on them.

There is nothing mysterious about the idea that the human mind in social. Emile Durkheim used the term "collective conscience," referring to the concepts and beliefs that are shared by a group of people. This does not mean that there is some kind of invisible mind hanging in the air over the group doing people's thinking for them; it is not a huge balloon floating in the sky beaming down messages. "Society" means nothing more than people interacting with each other; it is a process, not a thing. It happens whenever we meet. To say that the mind is social is only to say that our thinking is created, when we talk to each other. The concepts and ideas we have, and our feelings about which ideas are important, result from the conversations we have with each other. A person who knows how to talk, who has learned to carry on conversations, is a real human being. Once this ability exists, then comes the next step: each individual can think privately, inside his or her own mind, because *thinking is an internalized conversation*. Other kinds of human communication, such as reading and writing, are also spinoffs from this basic process of formulating shared ideas in conversations.

Now consider what we would like our computer to do. We want this computer to act as much as possible like a real human being. We don't want to start out by stuffing it with a file cabinet of information, or a set of rules about how to compute particular results from the data we put in. We want a computer that learns how to do things. It must be able to come up with new ideas. It should be flexible rather than rigid, able to deal with new situations as well as old ones. It shouldn't just solve problems; it should be able to invent and create; to make scientific discoveries, write literature, maybe even compose music. It should be able to make jokes, and to laugh at other people's jokes when they are funny.

This sounds like an impossibly tall order. After all, computer scientists have enough trouble developing a program that can carry out even one of the less creative tasks, let alone all these more complicated things. Still, it must be possible. We know that because human beings can do all these things. Of course, not everyone does all these things at once. But if it is true that human intelligence is social, then there is a particular kind of social interaction that underlies each of these kinds of thinking. Human beings who invent scientific theories are particular people who interact with other scientists; in fact we know quite a lot about the networks that put some scientists at the creative "hot spots" and others on the periphery where they do more routine work. The same is true of networks of musical composers or literary writers. The social world has many different regions: part of the sociological theory of intelligence, then, is the idea that where an individual is located in relation to other people is going to determine what kind of thinking he or she will do. It follows that if we want a computer that will be able to compose music or write novels, we are going to have to locate that computer in a social network of composers or novelists, and give the computer the ability to interact with those people so that it acquires both the skills and the motivations to do what they are doing.

Of course we can't program our computer all at once to do everything. We are going to have to start simple and build up to more complicated things. The fundamental thing that we need to construct is a computer that can interact with people. And then we are going to have to make it able to think when it is alone, to carry out the silent conversations "inside one's mind" that are carryovers from the conversations one holds outside with other people. We will have to give the computer some way of knowing who it prefers to talk to, and some way of motivating other people to spend time talking to it. In short, we need to make this computer just like an ordinary person making their way in the social world! Once we have that, we will have a way of making some ideas and concepts more important than others, so that the computer will have preferences as to what it likes to think about when it is alone. When we have this, sociology suggests, we will have a computer that can do all the things, from ordinary gossip and jokes up through highly creative thinking, that make up the range of human talent.

Such a computer program does not yet exist. What I am doing here is taking you to the frontiers of sociological theory. The sociology of mind has been developing in recent years, and this kind of theory is becoming more and more clearly formulated. As we will see, there are many practical problems in creating a computer that can implement sociological theory. But I am going to present you with a sketch of how sociologists are now thinking this can be done. I am inviting you to come along. Perhaps you will even end up becoming a sociologist of mind yourself, and make your own contributions to building a truly human artificial intelligence.

HOW TO PROGRAM A CONVERSATION

Here is the plan. First we will consider what we know about the sociology of conversation, and how we could make a computer that can go around talking to other people just like an ordinary human being. Then we will get the computer to think by itself, carrying out internal conversations inside its metallic "mind." Last we will consider what this computer will have to do to become a creative thinker, like a scientist or a novelist. I have already suggested that this will involve putting it into a particular kind of social network where this sort of creative thinking is done.

Let us imagine our computer. Let us call it SOCIO. As we will see, SOCIO is going to have to be more than a software program; it will need a body. It will be something like a robot, because as we shall see, there are certain bodily things that have to be done in social interactions. We want a model of social conversation, and that is going to involve not only what is said verbally, but how it is said, its emotional rhythm and tone and its accompanying nonverbal gestures.

TAKING TURNS AND KEEPING UP THE FLOW

For the last twenty years, sociologists have been studying conversations. Using tape recorders and sometimes video cameras, they have been able to look at what happens when people talk; sociologists have examined this at a level of detail that talkers themselves are hardly aware of. Once the conversation is captured on tape, it can be played back over and over again, and the tape slowed down to reveal things that happen in a fraction of a second. What have sociologists found from this research?

First of all, conversation is a process of turn-taking. One person talks, and then another one. This sounds obvious. But look at the process more closely. *One person talks at a time*, not two, not everybody. If two people are talking at once, we would say they are fighting over the floor. When this happens, their voices get louder and more aggressive; they get more emotional, until one person stops talking and lets the other one have the turn to talk. If this doesn't happen, then the conversation stops entirely and people leave.

Notice that we have found a typical sociological principle here: we find out what the normal structure is by what happens when it gets violated. We know normal conversation operates by one-person-at-a-time because the talk gets disrupted and people get upset if this is violated. Like Durkheim's method, which we have met in Chapter 4 in the discussion of crime, we find out what holds society together by looking at the places where it falls apart.

By the same method, we find another aspect of the turn-taking mechanism. *When one person stops talking, another person starts immediately.* If we look closely at the tape recordings of a smoothly flowing conversation, the timing is very sharp. At the end of each turn, the next person comes in right on the beat, as if it were a piece of music they are playing together with their voices. If a second person doesn't come in on time, there is a gap; and the conversationalists feel it as a gap. We call it an embarrassing pause. It feels uncomfortable; we feel like somebody ought to say something. Again there is an emotional reaction. The conversational emotion changes when this happens.

The amazing thing is that people recognize a pause when in fact it may be extremely short. In the ordinary rhythm of a smooth-flowing conversation, there is only a few tenths of a second or less between one turn and the next; in fact, the timing is often so close that we see on the tape recording that the last speaker overlaps with the first word of the next speaker. If there is a gap of about half a second, it is noticeable to the speakers; they feel like the conversation is not really flowing the way it should. And if the gap is longer, they may feel like there are whole minutes of awkward silence, when in fact the gap may be only about one or two seconds

What do we learn from this? First of all, the rhythms of conversation go very fast. We are aware of what happens at a level of tenths of seconds. Not that we are very acutely aware, not as if it were something that we explicitly calculate—but we are organized to keep up a flow that goes along in fractions of seconds, and we *feel* that things are going right or going wrong when this rhythm changes.

Another point is that each person must be monitoring the other in order to anticipate when his or her turn is going to end. That is why the next speaker can come in, right on the beat. How does one do this? Pretty certainly it is not a highly conscious calculation. It is more of a feel, a process of paying attention to what the other person sounds like as a voice rhythm comes near the end of a turn.

Perhaps the most important point is this: we feel it is important to keep the conversation flowing, and what we say is just a means of making this happen. In other words, what we say is less important than the fact that we can keep on saying something to each other. Conversation is a lot like singing: the words are there mainly so that we can keep singing the melody. This "singing together" constitutes a social relationship. Good friends are people who can keep up a long string of easily flowing conversations. They settle into a rhythm; their voices take on the tone of "having a good chat," "rapping together," or whatever slang term we use to express it. If we can turn off the meaning of the words for a moment while we analyze this—something analogous to watching a TV picture with the sound turned off—we can see them getting into an emotional flow done with their voices. They are humming along, punctuating each other's utterances with a "yeah" or an "uh-huh'" in the right place; laughing together or feeling concerned together, getting indignant about the same things, sharing the same moods and above all keeping up the beat.

Of course this doesn't happen in every conversation. Some combinations of people are better able to do this than are other combinations, which is why some people are better friends than others. Some conversations are short and practical and end when the business is done; some conversations try to be sociable but don't get going at all. This is why pauses and hassles in the turn-taking are so significant: they indicate how the social relationship is going. An awkward pause is awkward because it means we are having trouble finding something to say to each other, or because there is something beneath the surface that one of us wants to avoid talking about. If we do a lot of fighting over who has the floor, it means we can't get ourselves focussed on the same thing; it means we are in a struggle over who has higher status, who is dominant.

A conversation, then, is a social ritual of the sort described by Durkheim and Goffman, that we analyzed in Chapter 2. It assembles a group of people, focusses their attention, keeps up a common mood. In this case, the symbols that result from the ritual, and that symbolize the social relationship, are the words of the conversation. Just as in the case of the other social rituals, the symbols are on the surface, and they are carried along on the deeper level of emotional interactions beneath the surface. The striking thing about a conversational ritual is that we can measure the level of emotional solidarity in detail from moment to moment, by looking at the rhythms and sounds of the talk.

MAKING OUR COMPUTER KEEP UP
A CONVERSATION

Now let's bring in SOCIO, our social computer. How are we going to program SOCIO so that it will be able to carry out a conversation like a human being? Without worrying about the details, let us list several rules that SOCIO will follow:

Rule 1: *When someone else stops talking, say something immediately that will keep up the flow of conversation.*

This isn't as easy as it seems. For one thing, SOCIO is going to have to know when someone is about to stop talking, so that it can come in without wasting any time. So while the last person is speaking, SOCIO is going to have to be computing, figuring out what it is going to say when it gets a chance. In other words, SOCIO has at least two sub-tasks to perform here: (a) anticipating exactly when the turn is going to come, and (b) figuring out something to say that will fit. Let's fill in branch (a) first.

Rule 2: *Monitor the rhythm of the other person's speech; when he or she reaches the rhythm that typically comes just before the end of a turn, get ready to talk.*

How is SOCIO going to do this? It is going to need a device for analyzing voice rhythms; and it will need to remember which kinds of rhythms come at which points in a conversation. For the present, as we think about constructing SOCIO, we are not going to worry about questions of how to make the hardware operate; let us just assume that computer engineers will have to make some such device if SOCIO is going to be like a real human conversationalist. But notice that SOCIO cannot be just an ordinary piece of computer hardware; it is going to have to possess rhythm analyzers and some other "organs" too. SOCIO cannot be just an electronic brain with a keyboard or even a voice synthesizer attached; SOCIO is going to need the computer equivalents of bodily organs that produce and receive of emotions. In order to speak in a way that will be recognized as socially real by another human being, SOCIO must have the capability of producing rhythmic vocal expressions, so that another person can tune in to its rhythms too.

Giving SOCIO a rhythm-producing and rhythm-decoding box turns out to be important for another reason too. We want SOCIO to be able to get in tune with the way another person is talking. Voice rhythm is important not only at the end of a turn, but also throughout the utterance. Successful conversationalists adjust their voices into a common rhythm, and this is what helps build up a shared emotion. Let us give SOCIO another rule that will make it aim to keep up the level of attunement in a conversation:

Rule 3: *Monitor the other person's voice rhythms; when you take a turn, match your own rhythms to the rhythms you have just heard.*

In actuality, the rhythmic synchronization between speakers takes time to build up during the course of a conversation, like a musical crescendo. We are oversimplifying here by making SOCIO hit maximal rhythmic synchronization right away. A more complicated and accurate program would allow for a build-up of emotions. But let us take this as a first approximation and move on to the next point.

We still have point (b) left over. We have instructed SOCIO to say something, anything at all, in order to keep up the turn-taking and the emotional rhythm. But what are we going to have SOCIO say? After all, it has to use words that are appropriate to what has gone before. In real life, if someone says something in a conversation that bears no relation to what has been said before, people are surprised. It is off the wall; people react with "Huh?" or "Why do you bring that up?" SOCIO needs to know how to make things relevant.

Rule 4: *When your turn comes, take some part of the topic that has been talked about in the last few turns, and say something further about it.*

We are simplifying again here. In real life, a speaker usually has the opportunity to scan all the previous conversations they have had with the other person, and can reintroduce some topic related to something they once talked about. If asked "Why do you bring that up?" you can say "Remember what happened last week? . . . ." Another alternative is that you can talk about something that is happening in the surrounding situation where the conversation is taking place, along the lines of "Hey look!

Isn't that a rattlesnake?" We could program SOCIO to cover these alternatives too, but let us just sketch a shorter version.

Notice that SOCIO can't simply repeat what someone else has said. (Well, actually we could allow a small amount of this, such as when one person repeats something back as a question or to be ironic: "Irma was at the movies with [emphasis] *Arnold*??" But in fact this is a different emotional tone and rhythm that the original speaker used. We haven't got SOCIO up to this level yet.) SOCIO has to add something new to what has been said, since SOCIO has to fit the constraints of any other conversational speaker, such as being interesting as well as relevant. We must load up SOCIO with a certain amount of things to talk about.

ACQUIRING CULTURAL CAPITAL

Let us call these conversational topics *cultural capital*, or CC for short. There are three main ways that SOCIO can get cultural capital.

(4.i) We could just build it into the program. This is the easiest way to do it, but it would make SOCIO rather unnatural. It would make SOCIO rather repetitive after a while; after someone has talked to it a few times, it would begin to get boring. There is in fact a computer program structured like this, called RACTER (short for "raconteur," story-teller). RACTER can ask what your name is and for a few other pieces of personal information, but isn't capable of listening to what you have to say or of learning much from you. For the most part RACTER goes off on monologues, constructed by combining bits and pieces of things from its built-in memory:

RACTER: "Would you like to hear a story?"
AUDIENCE: "Yes."
RACTER: "Who should the story be about?"
AUDIENCE: "Dwight."
RACTER: "A hi-fi, house and van are important nevertheless

Dwight loved a conic section! To observe a car as an image or appearance in a revolting reflector enraged Dwight. Why a conic section? A theoretician might cry that a conic section is essential; angrily the theoretician yodels "the conic section is essential anyhow Dwight fantasizes of cottages and vans." Scary. Formidable. What is this? The theoretician croons of a conic section during the time that Dwight fantasizes of vans. Would Bill think about the passions of Dwight? Dwight now was arrogant. The theoretician indubitably was supercilious. But Bill cried to them "Do you follow me?" Bill commenced to speak of foxes and crows, even children or a cousin. Scary! Next question."

This is amusing at first, but the novelty wears off as the limits of RACTER's program become apparent. This is not a sufficient way to make a human conversation.

(4.ii) The second way that SOCIO can acquire cultural capital is by having it store up things from previous conversations. This is one of the things that real-life human beings do. We take things from conversation and repeat them in the next. So as long as SOCIO gets to talk to various people and not always the same person, it can circulate gossip, store up news, find out new facts, and introduce them into conversation with the next person it meets. And since we have given SOCIO an instruction to talk about things related to topics that have just been mentioned, SOCIO should be able to keep up its end of the conversation as long as the new people it talks to talk about some of the things that are connected to topics it has heard about in previous conversations. If we add a few other capacities to SOCIO, such as the ability to read the newspaper, watch television, perhaps go to the movies, then we can make it into a fairly successful chatterbox.

(4.iii) Now SOCIO can put out a reasonably authentic conversation, but it is missing one of the things that makes human beings interesting to each other. There is a third way it could acquire cultural capital: create new things to say out of the material that it has at its disposal. What is available consists of things that have just been said, plus things it remembers from past conversations. SOCIO might be given the ability to make new combinations. For instance, SOCIO could respond to the words the other person just uttered, and search its memory for words that rhyme with some of those syllables but that continue to make sense related in some degree to the topic that was talked about. This particular program would give SOCIO the ability to make puns. A better form of humor would emerge if SOCIO could search for remarks that have double meanings, and where both meanings have some relevance to the conversation. Without going into all the complications here, we could designate a sub-program to be built to give SOCIO a sense of humor. Then SOCIO could tell jokes; to go along with this, we would add a sub-program in which SOCIO had a brief emotional response to jokes that other people told: when it deciphered a double meaning, for instance, it would utter an accelerated rhythmic sound resembling laughing. (Laughing, incidentally, is one of the vocal utterances allowed to violate the turn-taking rule against overlap: in fact, people are most likely to laugh at the same time, and they laugh more intensely when their laughs are most closely synchronized. SOCIO would need some additional programming rules to reflect this.)

Can we design SOCIO so that it gets new ideas? A rough approximation for such a mechanism would be to have it combine pieces of different past and present conversations. It could look for contradictions between different things that it has heard, and then come up with statements that overcome these contradictions. It could extrapolate ideas by applying them to new circumstances. For the present, let us leave this part of SOCIO's program vague, since there are numerous technical issues that would have to be solved.[1] This is one area in which sociologists who do con-

---

[1] I have left out two vxery important issues. One is that people get new things to say from their own actions and the actions of other people around them. They talk about what they've been doing and what they have seen, and about what they want to do and what they want other people to do. SOCIO would need to have a set of social interests so that it could *do* things as well as talk, and it would need the ability to put these actions into words.

versation analysis could help with more research, since we don't
know very much about the situation in which people come up
with new things to say in conversations, as compared to just
recirculating old things.

A MOTIVATION TO TALK TO PEOPLE:
SEEKING EMOTIONAL ENERGY

Assume now that we have created SOCIO and that it can
follow all the rules we have laid out so far. SOCIO can monitor
rhythmic tones that other people make in talking, and it can
mimic those tones in its own voice. It knows how to keep up a
nicely coordinated flow of turn-taking. It is able to remember
things to talk about, and it can even create new things to say,
ranging from jokes to new ideas. What is missing? Is SOCIO
going to be able to hold conversations like any other human
being?

One more thing SOCIO needs is a motivation to talk to other
people. It has to be able to choose who it will try to talk to,
and how long it will go on talking with him or her. We can't
just program the computer to be a nonstop chatterbox, like
RACTER, that will talk to anybody as long as the computer remains switched on. This would be unrealistic. Human beings
prefer to talk to some people more than others. Some conversations are more useful or more interesting than others; some
people are better friends than others. So we need SOCIO to be

---

The second problem is that there are many ways the same thought can
be put into words ("Pass the butter"; "Would you mind passing the
butter?" "Butter, please"; etc.). SOCIO would need some kind of mechanism for transforming various expressions into one thought, and vice versa.
I would suggest that the first issue gives us an answer to the second issue:
if SOCIO knows the fundamental kinds of social actions, it will be able to
break down or build up speech acts that relate to these actions. But our
story of SOCIO is complicated enough as it is. For this introduction, I will
leave these questions aside.

able to choose which conversation it prefers and which ones it spends little time on.

. There is another side of the same coin. SOCIO has to be able to get other people to want to talk to it. SOCIO must be capable of "figuring out" how to make friends with people whom it finds most attractive; it must be able to make itself interesting to other people, to make them feel they are getting something positive out of talking to it. We can't just rely on the novelty that people feel in talking to a computer program, since that motivation soon wears off; and anyway we want SOCIO to be able to get along with people because it is like a human being, not because it is like a computer.

In fact SOCIO does not have to "figure out" how to make friends, in the sense of explicitly calculating what steps it will go through to make its conversations successful. For human beings, this happens mostly unconsciously and as the result of emotions. We already have some of the basic mechanisms built into the design of SOCIO. Remember, SOCIO can monitor the voice rhythms of the person it is speaking with, and it can modulate its own voice to imitate those rhythms. These voice rhythms are one of the main ways by which emotions are expressed; and one feels one's own emotions in one's voice. What we need to do is program SOCIO so that it can pick out the conversations in which it gets the most favorable flow of emotions. By the same token, SOCIO will be popular with other people if it provides favorable emotions for them.

There are of course quite a few different emotions. People feel love, joy, anger, fear, hatred, surprise, and many other things. If we are willing to make SOCIO quite complicated, we could try to build in a theory of how all these different emotions are produced. A sociological theory whould show how various emotions result from particular kinds of social situations. (Some theories of this sort are listed in the bibliography at the end of the book.) Fortunately, we can get by here with something simpler. Besides all these specific emotions, there is a general emotional level that

people always have. Let us call this *emotional energy*, or EE.
It is a dimension ranging from high to low.

At the high end, a person with lots of emotional energy is enthusiastic and energetic. He or she is full of confidence. Everything he or she does seems quick and spontaneous, because there is no need to hesitate over what they want to do. A person who is on a hiph EE level is flowing along an emotional stream. Other people who come into contact are swept along too. This happens because emotions are contagious. In a conversation, if the speakers can manage to focus closely on each other's stream of talk, their voice rhythms become synchronized; and whatever emotional tone is being conveyed in their talk becomes shared. So if one person has high EE, any other person who manages to keep up a smoothly flowing conversation with them will also get high EE.

Now let us drop to the opposite end of the EE scale. Here a person feels depressed. There is no spontaneity, no enthusiasm. This too is contagious. Talking with a depressed person is depressing. For this reason, other people don't like to talk to a low EE person if they can avoid it. The end result is to make a depressed person even more depressed.

Most people are neither at the very high nor the very low end of the EE spectrum. They are relatively up, or relatively down. Much of the time they may be at the middle of the scale. Here one doesn't even notice the level of emotional energy; it just seems normal. This does not mean there is no EE; if it weren't there, you would be depressed, and unable to do anything. Normal EE flows along at just the right level so that you can get through your ordinary business, your ordinary conversational dealings with people, without noticing anything in particular. It is only when we feel livelier than usual, or deader than usual, that we become aware of our mood.

One's EE level can fluctuate during the day. It fluctuates because people are raising or lowering their EE as the result of every conversation they take part in. This is the compass by which people steer their way through their daily life. They want to interact with the persons who raise their EE, and they want to stay away from persons who lower their EE. On a more fine-grained level, inside every conversation, each person wants to talk about the kinds of things that increase EE and to stay away from talk that lowers it.

This gives us a way to program SOCIO so that it has a motivation to interact with some people more than others, and to talk about some things rather than others.

First we must give SOCIO some rules by which EE is raised or lowered.

Rule 5: *If you can keep the flow of conversational turns going smoothly, emotional energy goes up. If there is trouble in keeping up the smooth flow of turns, emotional energy goes down.*

Now we have linked EE back to the turn-taking mechanism. People like a smooth flow of interaction. As we have already seen, for this to take place there must be a mutual focus on each other's voice rhythms, so that each person can anticipate when it is their turn to sing a verse in the conversational "song," and when they should join in by keeping the beat with an "uh-huh," "right on," "you said it," and when they come into unison with a laugh. Let us assume that the amount of rhythmic coordination is what gives people emotional energy. Conversely, when the flow they expect is disrupted, they experience one of the disruptive emotions, such as surprise, anger, or fear. And when there is little or no flow at all, their EE is drained, and they feel depressed.

Which people are going to be able to have more success in keeping up a smooth flow of conversational turns, and which people are going to fail at it? Rule 4 tells us that in each turn you must be able to add something onto the topics that went before. In other words, you need to add some cultural capital (CC) that is similar but not identical to the CC that has already been talked about. So people who are successful in keeping up a conversation have the right kind of CC; and they had to get this from talking to other people previously (as well as creating new things to talk about by recombining older CC). This means that how well you do in *this* conversation depends on the social network you have been in *previously*. SOCIO has the same problem everybody else does: it starts out in a social network and needs to use its network contacts to handle each new social interaction.

SOCIO can't be a fixed set of information; it has to shuttle CC around from one part of a social network to another. It has to be able to relate news, tell gossip, as well as make jokes and create new ideas that other people find interesting. If it does this well, it will be able to keep up a good flow in most of its new conversations; and this in turn will enable it to have a high level of emotional energy. The condition of SOCIO's emotions, though, is not guaranteed. If SOCIO encounters people (or other computers built just like itself) who have drastically different CC, it will not do very well at keeping up a conversational flow, and its EE will go down.

Programming SOCIO is already getting to be pretty complicated, so I will not spend time filling in all the ways that EE rises and falls. Successful or unsuccessful flows of conversational turns is one important way; it corresponds to the degree of success or failure in maintaining focus in an *interaction ritual*, as described in Chapter 2. There is another important mechanism that affects EE, but I will only mention it briefly here. Having power in an interaction raises one's EE; being subject to someone else's power lowers one's EE. We could write this as another rule for SOCIO: <u>Rule 5a:</u> *Giving orders to another person raises one's EE; taking orders lowers one's EE.* Accordingly, SOCIO would act like human beings and try to put itself in situations where it had power, and avoid situations where it lacks power. But then we would have to make SOCIO even more complicated, by giving it the ability to seek power; and we would have to spell out all the kinds of things that we have dealt with in Chapter 3. For our simpler version of SOCIO we will leave this aside.

<u>Rule 6:</u> *Monitor the amount of emotional energy that is*

coming from each conversation and from each topic in the con-
versation. Compare this with the emotional energy you have
been getting from the conversations you have had recently with
other people. If the emotional energy from the current conversa-
tion goes up, try to keep this conversation going. If it goes down,
bring this conversation to a close and look for someone else
who generates a higher level of emotional energy.

With this rule, we are ready to launch SOCIO out into the
world. It will look for people to talk to, and will spend the most
time with people who give it an EE boost, and will stay away
from people who cause an EE loss. The fate of SOCIO, however, is not really in its own hands, or should we say, in its own
chips. Its fate depends on where it has been in the social network
around it, and what social network it can meet next. If SOCIO
comes from a narrow social network where there isn't much to
talk about except perhaps gossiping about each other, it will
have a harder time if it moves into a new set of acquaintances
where the cultural capital is entirely different. SOCIO is going
to have to work at picking up new CC, or else other people won't
want to spend much time talking to it. SOCIO is going to be
subject to the market of social interactions, just like people are.
What it has to talk about depends on where it happens to be in
that network. And SOCIO's emotional level, too, is going to
depend on what happens to it in the network. Though SOCIO
is only a machine, it is going to be enthusiastic or depressed,
experiencing daily emotional levels that are up, down, or normal. It will move in one direction and away from another on the
basis of these emotions.

In real life, emotional energy only lasts for a while and then
fades. If you are all hyped up over something, the feeling lasts
for a few hours and then dissipates, unless something happens
to keep it going. If we write this as part of SOCIO's program
(Rule 6a: EE *drops off if it isn't replenished*), then SOCIO is
going to have to keep going out there and interacting to keep
up its emotional energy supply.

MAKING SOCIO THINK WHEN IT IS ALONE

Finally we have gotten to the point where we can solve our original problem. We want SOCIO to be able to think like a human being. In order to do this, we had to design SOCIO so that it could carry on normal conversations with people. Now we can have SOCIO carry on thinking in private, when no one else is around, or without telling other people what it is thinking. We can program this on the basis of the sociological principle that *thinking is internalized conversation.*

SOCIO has been getting two things from its conversations with other people, and these will make up the ingredients of the thinking it does on its own. It has been acquiring *cultural capital* and *emotional energy.* Let us stress one point about how they are combined. Cultural capital is charged with the amount of EE that it has been getting in social situations. It is as if each piece of CC is tagged with an emotional price-tag; this idea is worth this much EE. If you talked about politics in your recent conversations, and found that you were getting a good, enthusiastic flow of conversation about your political beliefs, then the EE price-tag of those political ideas is high. If you talked about classical music and found that nobody wanted to talk with you, that subject's EE price-tag is low. The particular price-tag depends on kinds of people you happen to have encountered, of course; and there can be very different EE prices for the same pieces of CC in a different social network somewhere else.

Now let's give SOCIO a few rules that will make it think like an ordinary human being.

Rule 7: *When no-one else is present, carry out an imaginary conversation using your stored-up cultural capital having the highest emotional energy levels.*

In other words, the ideas SOCIO is going to think about are those which have been socially most successful in recent interactions. If a recent conversation has been really exciting, its words actually seem to hang in your mind. You find yourself repeating pieces of what happened.

Rule 8: *After something emotionally exciting happens, seek out someone whom you can repeat it to in a conversation. If there is no one around at the moment, repeat it to yourself in an inner conversation.*

When some exciting event happens, positive or negative, you tend to seek out a friend to tell it to. "Wait 'til I tell Tanya about this!" A friend is someone who is on the same wavelength in terms of cultural capital; from past experience you know you can talk about this kind of thing with him or her. The same with SOCIO. If it cannot find someone who is its "friend" to repeat the events to, it will engage in thinking: carry out the conversation silently to itself, inside the circuits of its "mind."

PLANNING AHEAD

Some of our thinking is repeating conversations we have already had. But some of our thinking points forward rather than backward. We think about what we are going to do. If the most important things we have to do are our social relationships, then we will spend much of our time thinking about who we are going to encounter and what we will say to them. This is done more emotionally than consciously and explicitly. We already know that when a conversation is going on, each person has to monitor what the other person is saying so as to know when to come in right on time without missing a beat; and we do this more by tuning in to an emotional flow than by consciously thinking about what we are going to say. The same thing holds with the inner conversations that make up what goes on in your mind.

Of course, sometimes it is true that you make a special effort to plan out in advance what you are going to say. If you are going to an important job interview, you may try to rehearse a script

of what you will say. A boy about to ask a girl to go out with
him may ponder over what lines he will speak. But this kind of
planning usually makes people self-conscious, and it disturbs
the emotional flow of talk as it actually happens. The situations
go off best if people are unconsciously primed to say what will
fit well with what the other person is prepared to talk about.

So most of the time when someone plans ahead, the "planning" happens spontaneously. The idea of certain people comes
into your head. The words you would like to say to them pop into
mind and form into sentences. To make SOCIO do this, we write
the following:

Rule 9: *Keep a list of people you have talked to. Weigh each
name on the list by the amount of emotional energy you have
been getting from talking to them. When you search for people
to talk to, the names with the highest EE loading come up first.*

We could add some additional sub-programs here, such as
having SOCIO think about where this person is usually found
and how it can get to them. What is even more important for
personal thinking, though, is not so much the actual conversations that will happen as the purely mental conversation with
oneself. People who are always with other people will never
do any private thinking because they are always talking out
loud. If a person is doing a lot of private thinking, real conversations have to be held in abeyance; imaginary conversations are taking the place of real conversations. So if we want
SOCIO to think, we need to put it in situations where its desire
to converse with other people is frustrated. We need to give
SOCIO some privacy.

Rule 10: *If there is no one to talk to, go through the list of
past conversational partners and pull out the names with the
highest EE loading. Go through your repertoire of cultural capital
and make up a conversation on a topic that fits the topics you
have gotten the most EE from with that person.*

Now we have SOCIO carrying out imaginary conversations
with a specific person. Since the conversation is only imaginary,
the other person is not really saying anything; SOCIO has to

make up both sides of the conversation out of its own memory. No new CC is coming in. Cultural capital is being used up rather than increased. After a while SOCIO is going to get bored with this conversation, and its EE level will go down. SOCIO then has to think of a conversation with a different person. This too will eventually run down. This process will go on until SOCIO has an opportunity to talk to a real person, where there will be a real chance for the cultural capital and emotional energy to increase.

If this were all there is to it, we haven't been very successful with the kind of thinking we've made SOCIO do. We've gotten SOCIO to imagine conversations when it has no one to talk to. Like a real human being, SOCIO gets bored after a while and desires even more to talk to someone real. We wanted to create a computer that can come up with new ideas. Instead we have a computer that can make itself bored.

PROGRAMMING CREATIVE THINKING

Nevertheless, we have almost reached the point where we can add to SOCIO's program the ability to think creatively. What we have done so far is fairly realistic. Real human beings do get bored, and we wanted SOCIO to follow the same paths as any other human being. So how is it that people sometimes manage to have creative ideas?

We know some of the answer from sociological research on creative thinkers in science, philosophy, literature, and other fields. Creative persons are usually in a network that brings them into contact with other creative persons. Some parts of these networks often connect together teachers and pupils, both of whom are highly successful. Aristotle was the pupil of Plato; Wittgenstein was the pupil of Bertrand Russell. Nobel Prize winners are frequently the pupils of previous prize-winners. But in order to be creative one cannot simply imitate one's teacher; that makes one a follower, not an innovator. The network distributes cultural capital, but that is not all it is passing along. A creative person is someone who is getting high emotional energy out of creating new ideas. What the pupil is getting from a creative teacher is not just a stock of ideas, but some of that EE flow found within the teacher's own creativity.

If we want SOCIO to be creative, then, we need to put it in contact with teachers who are already creative. What else do we have to do? After all, famous teachers have lots of pupils, and only a few of them end up being creative in their own right. If we examine the networks around creative individuals, we find an additional pattern. They are in contact with other persons who in order to be creative one cannot simply imitate one's teacher; pupil contact takes place across the generations. This second aspect of the network brings together persons who are in the same generation. There is typically a circle of young innovators, a group of "young Turks" meeting together, working out ideas to overthrow the old ideas. These creative groups are found in all sorts of fields and at all periods in history. In ancient times, Socrates, who was Plato's teacher, had a large circle of young followers many of whom made their reputations just as Plato did. In literature, there are such groups as the three Brontë sisters, young and unknown, each writing her novel, several of which—*Jane Eyre and Wuthering Heights*, for example—turned out to be famous. In modern days, we could single out the group at Niels Bohr's institute at Copenhagen in the 1920s carrying out the revolution in modern atomic physics; or the team of Crick and Watson at the Cavendish laboratory in the 1950s rushing to make the discovery of DNA. So if we want SOCIO to be as creative as these famous philosophical or scientific innovators, we will have to introduce it into the circle in the intellectual world where the forefront problems are being discussed.

One more pattern stands out. These creative networks are usually competitive. Creative individuals typically have rivals. They race against each other for who is to make an innovation first, and for whose work will receive greater attention. Crick and Watson successfully won the DNA race against the already famous prize-winner Linus Pauling at Cal Tech, and also appropriated results from another laboratory in London. The pattern is found in literary creativity and in other fields as well. We started off this chapter mentioning Mary Shelley's *Frankenstein*; she wrote it while staying in a castle in Switzerland with Percy Shelley and Lord Byron, in a contest over who could write the best horror story.

To program SOCIO to be creative, it must be primed to do several things.

Rule 11: *Look for other people who have already been creative, and make contact with them.*

SOCIO may have to go to school, and get itself in the position of being a favorite pupil of a successful teacher. Or it can go to work, and become an apprentice in the labor of an inventor or scientist. Or SOCIO might just be lucky enough (like certain real-life persons) to run into these creative people. SOCIO can also get some of the cultural capital of creative persons by reading what they have written.

Rule 12: *Make contact with people who are working on the forefront problems, who are attempting to create something innovative.*

SOCIO needs to find the "Young Turks," the revolutionaries who are trying to overthrow the old ideas. If it can get in with them, its emotional energy will be given a boost. To be accepted by the others, SOCIO needs to become an idea-revolutionary itself. How is it going to do this?

Rule 13: *Construct a conversation that combines the cultural capital being used in several different groups, recombine the ideas so that the new narration makes sense out of all the different conversations simultaneously.*

Here we are having SOCIO do something inside its own internal conversation similar to what it did in Rule 4, when it took its turn to talk and added something new to what had been said before. In Rule 4, all that SOCIO had to do was to say something that hadn't been said yet in that particular conversation; it was okay for SOCIO to repeat something it had heard somewhere else, or had said previously to some other person. In Rule 4.iii we had SOCIO make new combinations out of the CC that had just been used, which could be as simple as making a joke by re-arranging the words. This is creative but at a very low level. Now we want SOCIO to make a creative recombination of cultural capital at a very high level. This means it must come out with a statement that makes sense to a very large network of people who are all concerned with the same kind of problem. SOCIO can do this by forming new sentences that draw on several separate networks, and that transform these separate conversations into one conversation. People who were dealing previously with separate problems now find they are dealing with parts of the same problem. The person (or even the computer SOCIO) who puts them together into a single pattern becomes a famous creator by changing the way that other people see them.

Creative thinking involves finding a way to combine separate pieces of CC into one pattern. This might involve coming up with a pattern that makes sense out of the data from different experiments in different laboratories: for instance, Crick and Watson's double helix structure for DNA. It might involve putting together elements from old ghost stories of mountain castles with new stories about living nerve-tissues that transmit electricity—in this case, the ingredients that went into Mary Shelley's *Frankenstein*. A successful work of creativity does not just look back to the old conversations from which its ingredients were taken; it looks forward to the new conversational network that gets formed as the result of the recombination. This is why the creative individual needs to have all these network contacts. The creator is someone who makes group alliances inside his or her mind, and hits on a pattern of CC which feels like it is going to be successful in establishing a very widespread conversation. Many hitherto separate groups of scientists will be convinced by a double-helix shaped DNA; large numbers of readers will be thrilled by Frankenstein's monster. The creative thinker is not just combining ideas; he or she is combining social groups.

To make SOCIO creative, then, we don't have to make this computer so very different from any other human being. But human beings vary a great deal in how creative they are. So will SOCIO vary. Whether SOCIO is a conformist or an innovator depends on what kind of social network we put it in. If we want SOCIO to be a genius, we can't do it simply by putting "genius" into its wiring. Remember, we started out to make SOCIO able to do what human beings can do. Since human beings are basically social, SOCIO is social. SOCIO has all the potentialities and limits that people have, and that means it depends on what kinds of social networks it has around it.

INTO THE FUTURE

We haven't really built SOCIO, of course. I have only sketched out in very broad terms the kinds of programs we would have to put into a computer if it were to begin to be something like a human being. There are many difficult problems to be solved in implementing this general model into a working program. Nevertheless, if sociological theory is correct, the only way that we are ever going to build such a thinking computer is by following something like this plan.

Even if we never build SOCIO, just thinking about it has been useful. Imagining SOCIO has made us consider just what are the social processes that enable us to interact with each other. It reveals what it is we do when we carry on a conversation, and what is happening when we hold the inner conversations that make up our thinking. It makes us focus on the special kinds of social networks and inner conversations that result in creative thinking. We can continue to learn something about sociology by imagining how to build SOCIO, even if it never comes about.

Personally, I think that eventually we will build SOCIO. The futuristic "space age" does not suddenly arrive all at once. It already started years ago, and has been advancing bit by bit. It has come about in part by applying older sciences, in part by creating new sciences. One of those new sciences, artificial intelligence, is just in its infancy. It will become stronger as it makes an alliance with a science not so very much older, i.e., social science. As we learn more about interaction rituals and emotional energy, about the flow of cultural capital through social networks, it is going to become more and more possible to build SOCIO.

Will SOCIO be a good thing to have? Mary Shelley's *Frankenstein* suggests that it won't. But maybe we have these fears because we haven't thought about it carefully enough. For one thing, SOCIO doesn't have to be built like a giant Frankensteinian monster, capable of strangling people with one hand. SOCIO in fact is designed to be like just another ordinary human being. So our question really is: are human beings good or bad? We are designing SOCIO to seek for emotional energy in interactions with people, by attempting to keep up the same emotional wave length with them. Frankenstein's monster really wanted love; it became destructive when it didn't get it from people. Here too SOCIO may teach us something about ourselves.

AFTERWORD

There is much more that could be said. Every topic that has been opened up here can be taken much further. And there are many other areas in sociology where the ideas and the findings are far from obvious. I have scarcely touched upon larger social structures, such as the way in which organizations mesh with their technologies and their environments, or the large-scale causes of political revolutions. Sociologists researching such topics are still turning up new and unexpected findings.

The same can be said of the structures within which we ourselves are embedded. Sociology is uncovering many once-hidden aspects of the professions we encounter in daily life and of the working of the system of stratification of which we are a part. The educational system itself is now appearing to us in a paradoxical new light. And at a much more fine-grained microlevel of sociological study, new perspectives are being turned up. We are finding a deeper structure in the way ordinary language works, and the ways emotions and nonverbal communications mold our immediate social experiences.

If I do not go into further details about these discoveries, it is largely to entice you into pursuing sociology for yourself. It may not always be easy as the best and most interesting parts of sociology are not always the most prominently displayed. Textbooks often have a way of burying the significant questions un-

der banal illustrations and conventionally obvious explanations.
Still, you can always orient yourself to the deeper and more exciting issues by continually reminding yourself of a few questions.

Supposing a given pattern is reported as a fact. Why is it
like this instead of like something else? Don't take the current
family structure for granted, or anything else for that matter.
Why does it take this form rather than another? Any explanation that implies that it is natural, or functional for the preser-
vation of society, or is that way because the culture decrees it to
be so—such explanations are really no explanation at all. The
only way to truly get a grip on the issue is to look for variations:
find where in fact the family system has been different, say, and
then try to compare conditions to find what does make for the
differences. The method can be used for everything. It does not
always make for easy answers, but at least it opens up our questioning and gets us away from the too-obvious and taken-for-
granted solutions.

You can always judge whether there is anything more of interest to be said about a topic by asking whether the explanation has the force of generality. Do we know enough about this
social institution so that we can say when and why it will take
this particular form, and when it will take another? Do we have
only a description of the way things are now, or can we say
what would change it into something different in the future?
Only if we can answer, yes, to these questions, can we say that
the topic is mastered and there is no more exploration to be
done.

Clearly sociology is still far from this goal. But at any rate
we have gotten beneath the surface, and we know something
about the directions in which to move. We have already seen
some of the keys that will open those doors that lie ahead. We
know that the patterns of rationality lie on the surface of ap-
pearances, and that in order for people to be rational they have
to operate within certain socially given limits. We know that
much of what shapes people's behavior lies beyond the lighted

circle of our focused consciousness, in the penumbra of the taken-for-granted.

When we look for the keys to social organization and social power, it is here that we find many of the prime determinants. We have seen that power resides to a large degree with those persons who are closest to the areas of uncertainty in the social world. Their power comes from being able to interpret these unknown contingencies to other people who merely follow social routines. Social organization itself rests heavily upon those nodes where people come together in ritualistic ways. It is the ritual aspect of things that produces solidarity; just how tightly groups are knitted together follows from how ritualized are their usual social encounters. Because of this, many of our most strongly believed ideas are symbolic rather than practical: they represent to us membership in our group. That is the reason why they are so inadequate if we try to use them merely as rational tools by which to understand the world around us.

The larger structures of society are built up out of aggregations of these ritually founded groups. The combination of groups is often full of conflict, with different groups pushing and tugging at each other for economic precedence and social power, as well as to impose their own moral and symbolic ideas upon the others. We have looked briefly at one result of this, in the area of crime. Such structural patterns as this often have an ironic tinge. With sufficient sociological detachment, we can see that the social structure is constantly manufacturing crime. At the same time, we see that crime itself is a form of social organization and hence is subject to the same limitations as everything else. We seem not to be able to control crime, but crime tends to suffer its own imperfections and confines itself within its own boundaries.

Looking at the family, too, we have seen the way in which various structures mesh together to grind out the recent patterns of change. Economic and erotic property relations affect the power of men and women both at home and in the outside world of work, and the shifting battlelines in one sphere inevitably shift the lineup of contending forces in the other. All this is carried out, as human arrangements always are, largely beneath the surface of our usual thoughts and feelings. But our changing feelings about love and sex themselves symbolize and ritualize these changes in the structure of power between the sexes.

In the case of the family and of the position of women in society, we see at any rate one area where the sociological outlook is not necessarily pessimistic. We have become used to sociological ironies; nothing works the way it should. But in one area at least, the larger structural movement now under way may indeed be favorable to a greater sum of human happiness in the future. The world of the past was no ideal, however much some people may romanticize it; by comparison, the long-term trend shows some positive possibilities.

The best of sociology is like a hidden treasure chest. Most people don't know much sociology beyond the most obvious. Most of us know some pop sociology, such as the existence of problems like poverty and racial and gender inequality. We all know bureaucracies are a nuisance but we don't know why they come to be that way. Pop sociology knows how to describe today's society but not how to explain why these patterns exist. Nonobvious sociology pulls some insights out of the treasure chest, letting us see the underlying conditions that are moving us, and giving us the chance to steer our course instead of just blindly drifting. There are little opportunities as well as big ones to put sociological insight to work. Heady analysts who want to understand the stock market or the interlocks between businesses are turning to sociology. So are the most advanced cognitive scientists trying to create artificial intelligence. As our world becomes more sophisticated, nonobvious sociology is going to be a growing part of its future.

BIBLIOGRAPHY

Sources for the materials in the preceding chapters are given here. The reader interested in pursuing these topics further might begin with these, and follow up the references found in them.

1. THE NONRATIONAL FOUNDATIONS OF RATIONALITY

The basic argument about the nonrational foundations of society comes from Émile Durkheim, *The Division of Labor in Society*, originally published in 1893 (New York, Free Press, 1964). A quite different version of essentially the same point is made by Harold Garfinkel, *Studies in Ethnomethodology* (Englewood Cliffs, N.J.: Prentice-Hall, 1967). The free-rider problem was stated by Mancur Olson, *The Logic of Collective Action* (Cambridge: Harvard University Press, 1965). The experiment referred to in the text concerning the Kitty Genovese murder is described in John M. Darley and Bibb Latané, "Bystander intervention in emergencies: diffusion of responsibility," *Journal of Personality and Social Psychology 8* (1968): 377–83. Recently sociologists following the "rational choice" perspective have attempted to find a solution to the "free-rider problem"; these include authors Michael Hechter, *Principles of Group Solidarity* (Berkeley: University of California Press, 1987), and James S. Coleman, *Foundations of Social Theory* (Cambridge: Harvard

189

University Press, 1990). Both Hechter and Coleman tried to show
that it is rational for persons to institute normative controls over
each other, if they can monitor each other and communicate
effectively over who is conforming and who is violating the
norms. Still, these theories have to assume that persons are
sensitive to each others' opinions, thereby implying some emotional ties between them.

Max Weber's theory of bureaucracy and his discussion of
functional and substantive rationality are in *Economy and Society*, originally published 1922 (New York: Bedminster Press,
1968, pp. 85–86, 956–1005).. Karl Mannheim developed the
argument in *Man and Society in an Age of Reconstruction*,
originally published 1935 (New York: Harcourt, Brace, 1940).
C. Wright Mills applied it to American government in *The
Power Elite* (New York: Oxford University Press, 1956), and
The Causes of World War III (New York: Simon and Schuster,
1958). Karl Marx's classic theory of the nature of capitalism and
its contradictions are given in *Capital*, originally published 1867–
93 (Chicago: C. H. Kerr, 1906–9), and *Grundrisse*, original
manuscript 1857–58 (New York: Random House, 1973). Some
of its important modern versions are Paul A. Baran and Paul M.
Sweezey, *Monopoly Capital* (New York: Monthly Review Press,
1966), and James O'Connor, *The Fiscal Crisis of the State* (New
York: St. Martin's Press, 1973). There are many sociological
analyses of how policies designed for one purpose end up having
quite different effects. One of these, concerning the American
educational system, is Randall Collins, *The Credential Society*
(New York: Academic Press, 1979).

The contrast between traditional and modern ways of doing
business is central to Weber's theory of the rise of capitalism.
His most famous discussion is *The Protestant Ethic and the
Spirit of Capitalism*, originally published 1904–5 (New York:
Scribner's, 1930), although the reader should be aware that this
was his first book on the subject and only the tip of the iceberg
that constituted his later theory. Weber's complete model is
given in *General Economic History*, originally published 1923

(New York: Collier-Macmillan, 1961), and in Randall Collins, "Weber's Last Theory of Capitalism: a Systematization," *American Sociological Review* 45 (1980): 925–42. The ceremonial, non-market form of tribal economy is described in Marcel Mauss, *The Gift*, originally published 1925 (New York: Norton, 1967), and Karl Polanyi (ed.), *Trade and Market in the Early Empires* (Glencoe: Free Press, 1957). The atmosphere of distrust that characterized medieval societies can still be found today in traditional areas like Sicily, described in Edward Banfield, *The Moral Basis of a Backward Society* (New York: Free Press, 1958).

Since the state can enforce contracts, the question of what holds the state together is an important one. Weber gives his analysis in *Economy and Society*, pp. 212–99 and 901–1157. Marx's best political analysis is in *The Eighteenth Brumaire of Louis Bonaparte*, originally published 1852 (New York: International Publishers, 1963); I have tried to synthesize their arguments in *Conflict Sociology* (New York: Academic Press, 1975, ch. 7). Ralf Dahrendorf, in *Class and Class Conflict in Industrial Society* (Stanford: Stanford University Press, 1959) shows that any organization having order-givers and order-takers generates a struggle over power. The theory of how groups become mobilized into conflict when they have the resources to become organized is given by Charles Tilly, *From Mobilization to Revolution* (Reading, Mass.: Addison-Wesley, 1978). The area of group conflicts is overviewed by James B. Rule, *Theories of Civil Violence* (Berkeley: University of California Press, 1988). An application of conflict theory to predicting the communist revolutions of the 1980s is Randall Collins, "The Future Decline of the Russian Empire," pp. 186–209, in *Weberian Sociological Theory* (Cambridge: Cambridge University Press, 1986).

2. THE SOCIOLOGY OF GOD

Durkheim's classic analysis of religion and ritual is in *The Elementary Forms of the Religious Life*, originally published 1912

(New York: Collier-Macmillan, 1961). His theory that different types of societies will have different sorts of moralities is given in *The Division of Labor in Society*. More precise evidence on this has been calculated in Guy E. Swanson, *The Birth of the Gods* (Ann Arbor, University of Michigan Press, 1962), followed up by Ralph Underhill, "Economic and Political Antecedants of Monotheism: a Cross-Cultural Study," *American Journal of Sociology* 80 (1975): 841–61; and John H. Simpson, "Sovereign Groups, Subsistence Activities, and the Presence of a High God in Primitive Societies," in Robert Wuthnow (ed.), *The Religious Dimension* (New York: Academic Press, 1979). Other versions of the theory of correspondence between religious symbols and social structures are in Claude Lévi-Strauss, *Structural Anthropology* (New York: Basic Books, 1963), and Talcott Parsons, *Societies: Comparative and Evolutionary Perspectives* (Englewood Cliffs, N.J.: Prentice-Hall, 1967). A good description of the main varieties of human societies throughout world history is Gerhard Lenski, *Power and Privilege* (New York: McGraw-Hill, 1966).

Max Weber's analyses of religion and social change, besides those referred to in the bibliography for chapter 1, include *The Religion of China*, originally published 1916 (Glencoe: Free Press, 1951), *The Religion of India*, originally published 1916–17 (Glencoe: Free Press, 1958), and *Ancient Judaism*, originally published 1917–18 (Glencoe: Free Press, 1952). Marx's treatment of religion as ideology may be found in *The German Ideology*, originally published 1846 (New York: International Publishers, 1947).

Durkheim's ideas about ritual were applied to tribal societies by a group of British social anthropologists, especially Arthur Radcliffe-Brown and W. Lloyd Warner. Warner came to the United States to study the ritual and organization of a modern community; the most striking result of this is *The Living and the Dead* (New Haven: Yale University Press, 1959). One of Warner's students was Erving Goffman, who opened up an entirely new kind of analysis of rituals by applying it to the little polite (and impolite) actions of everyday life in *The Presenta-*

tion of Self in Everyday Life (New Work: Doubleday, 1959), and *Interaction Ritual* (New York: Doubleday, 1967). Others of Goffman's important works are *Strategic Interaction* (Philadelphia: University of Pennsylvania Press, 1969), which shows how people in conflict take advantage of each other's nonrational vulnerabilities, and *Frame Analysis* (New York: Harper and Row, 1974). I have developed the general theory of rituals in *Conflict Sociology*, chapters 3 and 4, and more recently in my *Theoretical Sociology* (San Diego: Harcourt, Brace, Jovanovich, 1988), chapter 6.

3. PARADOXES OF POWER

The comparison of monetary, coercive, and normative controls comes from Amitai Etzioni, *A Comparative Analysis of Complex Organizations* (New York: Free Press, 2nd ed., 1976). Other classic analyses of the difficulties of control in organizations are Melville Dalton, *Men Who Manage* (New York: Wiley, 1959), and Donald Roy, "Quota restriction and goldbricking in a machine shop," *American Journal of Sociology* 57 (1952): 427–42. The weakness of coercive controls in psychological experiments was pointed out by B. F. Skinner, *Science and Human Behavior* (New York: Macmillan, 1953); R. L. Solomon argues its effectiveness as a purely negative control, to prevent people from doing things rather than to motivate them to do something positive in Solomon, "Punishment," *American Psychologist* 19 (1964): 239–52. I have given a formal statement of organizational control theory in *Theoretical Sociology*, chapter 13.

Harold Garfinkel's bizarre experiments to demonstrate the importance of what is inexpressible and taken-for-granted are described in *Studies in Ethnomethodology*. This line of analysis is expanded by Aaron Cicourel, *Cognitive Sociology* (Baltimore: Penguin Books, 1973). Goffman presents his own version of this process in *Frame Analysis*. Within organization theory, the analogous problem of optimizing versus satisficing was first formu-

lated by James G. March and Herbert A. Simon, *Organizations*
(New York: Wiley, 1958). It has been taken up more recently
by Oliver Williamson, *Markets and Hierarchies* (New York:
Free Press, 1975), which draws on Goffman's ideas as well. The
power of those people who control areas of uncertainty is demonstrated by Harold L. Wilensky, *Intellectuals in Labor Unions*
(Glencoe: Free Press, 1956); Wilensky, "The Professionalization
of Everyone?" *American Journal of Sociology* 70 (1964): 137–58;
and by Michel Crozier, *The Bureaucratic Phenomenon* (Chicago: University of Chicago Press, 1962). A later statement of
the general problem is Samuel B. Bacharach and Edward Law-
ler, *Power and Politics in Organizations* (San Francisco: Jossey-
Bass, 1980).

4. The Normalcy of Crime

The changing history of fashions in punishments is given in Mi-
chel Foucault, *Discipline and Punish* (New York: Pantheon
Books, 1977), and Graeme Newman, *The Punishment Response*
(New York: Lippincott, 1978). The classic statement of the
theory of deviant lower-class group cultures is in Edwin H.
Sutherland and Donald R. Cressey, *Principles of Criminology*
(New York: Lippincott, 1955). Organized crime as a mode of
social mobility for Italian immigrants is analyzed in Daniel Bell,
The End of Ideology (New York: Free Press, 1961). Albert
K. Cohen, *Delinquent Boys: The Culture of the Gang* (Glencoe:
Free Press, 1955) argued that the school itself motivated non-
achievers into becoming delinquents.

There are a variety of criticisms of the conservative and liberal theories of crime. Travis Hirschi, *Causes of Delinquency*
(Berkeley: University of California Press, 1969), shows that there
are no differences in delinquency rates by social class background. Daniel Glaser. *The Effectiveness of Prison and Parole
System* (Indianapolis: Bobbs-Merrill, 1969) shows the general
ineffectiveness of prisons. Theodore Sellin's' articles in H. Bedau
(ed.), *The Death Penalty in America* (Chicago: Aldine, 1967)

shows that there is no difference in the murder rates when the death penalty is abolished, Jack P. Gibbs, *Punishment and Deterrence* (New York: Elsevier, 1970), however, presents some evidence that the certainty of punishment rather than its severity is the crucial factor in whether it has any deterrent effect.

The labeling theory of crime is due especially to Howard S. Becker, *Outsiders: Studies in the Sociology of Deviance* (New York: Free Press, 1963). Becker introduced the concept of "moral entrepreneurs" who create new crime categories. A similar study, of the Prohibitionist movement, is Joseph R. Gusfield, *Symbolic Crusade: Status Politics and the American Temperance Movement* (Urbana: University of Illinois Press, 1963). The labeling theory has been criticized by Hirschi, *Causes of Delinquency*, and others. A discussion of how prohibition of drugs and gambling creates ancillary crimes is Thomas C. Schelling, "Economic Analysis of Organized Crime," in *Task Force Report: Organized Crime* (Washington, D.C.: Government Printing Office, 1967). The concept of victimless crime was made prominent by Edwin M. Schur, *Crimes Without Victims* (Englewood Cliffs, N.J.: Prentice-Hall, 1965). A wealth of information and analysis of the behavior of police, including plea-bargaining and clearance rates, are in Jerome K. Skolnick, *Justice Without Trial* (New York: Wiley, 1966), and Donald Black, *The Manners and Customs of the Police* (New York: Academic Press, 1980).

Radical theories of crime as the result of class conflict are given in Richard Quinney, *The Social Reality of Crime* (Boston: Little, Brown, 1970). Crime in socialist societies is analyzed in Walter D. Connor, *Deviance in Soviet Society* (New York: Columbia, University Press, 1972). Illegal practices in the Russian economic system are described in J. S. Berliner, *Factory and Manager in the U.S.S.R.* (Cambridge: Harvard University Press, 1957).

The experience of Denmark without a police force in 1944 is described in J. Andenaes, "General Prevention: Illusion or Reality?" *Journal of Criminal Law, Criminology and Police Science* 43 (1952): 176–98. Very revealing statistics on crime, including victimization surveys, are in various government publications, especially U.S. Department of Justice, *Source Books of Criminal Statistics* (appears annually). See also the annual *Statistical Abstract of the United States.*

Durkheim's theory of crime is given in *The Rules of the Sociological Method*, originally published 1895 (Chicago: University of Chicago Press, 1938). The theory was applied to colonial America by Kai T. Erikson, *Wayward Puritans* (New York: Wiley, 1966). The theory of violence and punishment as ritual for maintaining boundaries of stratified groups is stated in Randall Collins, "Three Faces of Cruelty," *Sociology Since Midcentury* (New York: Academic Press, 1981). On the difficulties of making a successful criminal career, see the classic study by Edwin H. Sutherland, *The Professional Thief* (Chicago: University of Chicago Press, 1937).

5. LOVE AND PROPERTY

The theory of sexual stratification was begun in the late nineteenth century by Friedrich Engels, *The Origin of the Family, Private Property, and the State*, originally published 1884 (New York: International Publishers, 1972). Max Weber also made important remarks on the subject in *Economy and Society*, pp. 356–69. The concept of sexual property goes back to Kingsley Davis, "Jealousy and Sexual Property," *Human Society* (New York: Macmillan, 1949), and Claude Lévi-Strauss, *The Elementary Structures of Kinship*, originally published 1949 in French (Boston: Beacon Press, 1969). I have developed these into a comparative theory of the variations in sexual stratification in *Theoretical Sociology*, chapter 5.

Anthropological evidence on the varieties of sexual arrangements and family systems may be found in Jack Goody, *Comparative Studies in Kinship* (Stanford: Stanford University Press, 1969), and Robin Fox, *Kinship and Marriage* (Baltimore: Penguin Books, 1967). The classic paper on the sexual marketplace in American society is Willard Waller, "The rating and dating complex," *American Sociological Review* 2 (1937): 727–34. The incest taboo and generational property are described in the works above by Lévi-Strauss, Goody, and Fox; I give a fuller analysis of it in "Lévi-Strauss' Structural History," *Sociology Since Mid-century* (New York: Academic Press, 1981). Historical studies of the changing family since the middle ages are Philippe Aries, *Centuries of Childhood* (New York: Random House, 1962), and Lawrence Stone, *The Family, Sex and Marriage in England, 1500–1800* (New York: Harper and Row, 1977). Historical shifts in the concept of love are described in Denis de Rougement, *Love in the Western World* (New York: Pantheon, 1956).

The most important analyses of the economic organization of the household have been done by. Marxist-oriented feminists. The classic statement is Juliet Mitchell, *Woman's Estate* (New York: Vintage Books, 1971). A recent overview of theories is Janet Saltzman Chafetz, *Feminist Sociology: an Overview of Contemporary Theories* (Itasca, Ill.: Peacock, 1988). Among the most comprehensive recent theories is Janet Chafetz, *Gender Equity. An Integrated Theory of Stability and Change* (Newbury Park, Calif.: Sage, 1988). Evidence on the position of women in soviet societies is given by Michael Paul Sacks, "The Place of Women," in Jerry G. Pankhurst and Michael Paul Sacks, *Contemporary Soviet Society* (New York: Praeger, 1980). That the relative domestic power of wives depends upon the relationships between their income and their husbands was first shown in Robert Blood and Donald Wolfe, *Husbands and Wives* (New York; Free Press, 1960). Philip Blumstein and Pepper Schwartz, *American Couples* (New York: William Morrow, 1983) have shown that the balance of power based on money and position in the sexual marketplace exists not only among married partners but also among gay couples.

Data on the changing patterns of premarital sexual behavior can be found by comparing the data in the Kinsey reports, *Sexual Behavior in the Human Male; Sexual Behavior in the Human Female* (Philadelphia, Saunders, 1948, 1952), with later data in John DeLamater and Patricia MacCorquodale, *Premarital Sexuality* (Madison: University of Wisconsin Press, 1979). The changing birth rates, abortion rates, and marriage and divorce rates can be followed in *Statistical Abstract of the United States* (U.S. Government Printing Office: annually). On traditionalist, pro-family movements, one study is Louis Zurcher and George Kirkpatrick, *Citizens for Decency: Antipornography Crusades as Status Defence* (Austin: University of Texas Press, 1976). Studies of the social bases of the abortion controversy include Kristin Luker, *Abortion and the Politics of Motherhood* (Berkeley: University of California Press, 1984), which profiles social backgrounds of the women in the opposing camps; Faye D. Ginsberg, *Contested Lives: The Abortion Debate in the American Community* (Berkeley: University of California Press, 1989); and Michelle Condit, *Decoding Abortion Rhetoric: Communicating Social Change* (Urbana: University of Illinois Press, 1990). The analysis of open marriages was suggested to me by Professor Paul Vogt of the State University of New York at Albany. I owe the analysis of the future of love marriages to Professor Samuel Kaplan of Boston University.

6. Can Sociology Create an Artificial Intelligence?

A good review of efforts to build an Artificial Intelligence, and of the problems encountered, is Alan Wolfe, "Mind, Self, Society and Computer: Artificial Intelligence and the Sociology of Mind," *American Journal of Sociology* 96 (1991): 1073–96. The classic theory of mind as internalized conversation is George Herbert Mead, *Mind, Self and Society* (Chicago: University of Chicago Press, 1934). Turn-taking in conversation was first analyzed by Harvey Sacks, Emanuel A. Schegloff, and Gail Jefferson, "A simplest systematics for the organization of turn-taking for conversation," *Language* 50 (1974): 696–735. More recent developments in sociological conversation analysis can be found in J. Maxwell Atkinson and John Heritage, *Structures of Social Action. Studies in Conversation Analysis* (New York: Cambridge

University Press, 1984); Deirdre Boden and Don H. Zimmerman, *Talk and Social Structure* (Cambridge, England: Polity Press, 1991); and Allen D. Grimshaw, *Conflict Talk* (New York: Cambridge University Press, 1990). Some ways in which microsociological research can contribute to artificial intelligence are discussed in the essays in C. Nigel Gilbert and Christian Heath (eds.), *Social Action and Artificial Intelligence* (Aldershot, England: Gower, 1985).

A general overview of micro-sociological theories of interaction, the mind, and conversation is found in Randall Collins, *Theoretical Sociology* (San Diego: Harcourt, Brace, Jovanovich, 1988). Chapters 6 to 9. The cutting edge of research and theory in the sociology of emotions can be found in Theodore D. Kemper (ed.), *Research Agendas in the Sociology of Emotions* (Albany: SUNY Press, 1990); and in Thomas Scheff, *Microsociology, Discourse, Emotion and Social Structure* (Chicago: University of Chicago Press, 1990). My theory of people going through a series of *interaction ritual chains* was first presented in "On the Microfoundations of Macro-sociology," *American Journal of Sociology* 86 (1981): 984–1014. The theory of thinking as internalized interaction rituals carried along on emotional energies is presented in my paper "Toward a Neo-Meadian Sociology of Mind," *Symbolic Interaction* 12 (1989): 1–31.

Bruno Latour, *Science in Action* (Cambridge: Harvard University Press, 1987), gives a beautifully written explanation of how science is constructed by social networks. The model of how creative thinkers are located in competitive networks of other leading thinkers is developed in Randall Collins, "A Micro-Macro Theory of Creativity in Intellectual Careers," *Sociological Theory* 5 (1987): 47–69, and in "Toward a Theory of Intellectual Change: the Social Causes of Philosophies," *Science, Technology and Human Values* 14 (1989): 107–140.

INDEX

CPSIA information can be obtained at www.ICGtesting.com
Printed in the USA
BVOW07s1747261114

376814BV00001B/2/P